A COMPREHENSIVE GUIDE TO WILDERNESS & TRAVEL MEDICINE

ERIC A. WEISS, M.D., F.A.C.E.P.

The Choice of Outdoor Professionals Worldwide

Published by Adventure Medical Kits
P.O. Box 43309, Oakland, CA 94624

Printed in the United States of America
First Edition November, 1992
Second Edition July, 1997
Third Edition July, 2005

Illustrations: Rod Nickell, Danny Sun, Butch Collier,
and Patricia A. Jacobs
Book Design and Layout: Dan Armstrong and Russ Fry
Primary Editor: Nis Kildegaard
Cover Photo: Lannie Johnson
Thomserku Peak in the Himalaya, Nepal

Library of Congress Catalog-in-Publication Data
Weiss, Eric
A Comprehensive Guide to Wilderness & Travel Medicine
by Eric A. Weiss – 3rd Edition
ISBN 0-9659768-1-5
1. Wilderness First-Aid 2. Travel Medicine
3. Backpacking First-Aid 4. Wilderness Survival

DEDICATION

This book is dedicated to Amy and Danny Weiss — my two favorite indoor and outdoor companions.

This book is also dedicated to my mother and father for their steadfast support and unconditional love. They have unselfishly devoted their lives to the health and happiness of their children.

Finally, I'd like to dedicate this edition to the memory of Oscar V. Lopp. As the Director of the Sierra Club's Mountain Medical Institute, Oscar introduced more people to wilderness medicine than any other human. He had an extraordinary level of energy, a contagious sense of humor, and an indomitable spirit.

ACKNOWLEDGMENTS

I'd like to thank and acknowledge my close friends and colleagues in wilderness medicine, Howard Donner, M.D., Lanny Johnson, FNP/PA, Paul Auerbach, M.D., Peter Hackett, M.D., Gene Allred, M.D., Robert Norris, M.D., Findlay Russell, M.D., Joe Serra, M.D., Henry Herrman, D.D.S., Jim Bagian, M.D., Tim Erickson, M.D., and Gary Kibbee for their companionship, inspiration, and guidance.

Eric A. Weiss, M.D., F.A.C.E.P.

PREFACE

This book goes far beyond traditional first aid and embraces a new philosophy in wilderness medicine education. It brings to fruition a juxtaposition of more than 10 years of research, clinical experience, and teaching into a powerful guide for those who travel far from modern civilization. Revolutionary advances in emergency medicine knowledge, techniques, and equipment, as well as a new standard of first-aid practice, permeate the text and provide the foundation for lay people to provide vital emergency care in remote settings.

This book is also unique in that it specifically addresses the components included in most Adventure Medical Kits when discussing the treatment of medical emergencies, and it introduces a myriad of improvised techniques that empower the reader to provide meaningful emergency care, even when first-aid materials are not readily available.

The information in these pages is intended to help you manage medical emergencies in remote environments when professional medical care or rescue is not readily available. It is not a substitute for taking a comprehensive first-aid or wilderness medicine course, or for seeking prompt medical care in the event of an illness or accident. Whenever someone becomes ill or injured, obtaining professional medical attention should take priority after administering appropriate first aid. The reader should use this book for guidance in difficult and remote situations only and should not attempt to perform any procedure that he is not comfortable with or trained to render, unless the victim will die without that intervention. Legally, a rescuer is always liable for his own actions and should never take any unnecessary risks or perform any medical procedure unless it is absolutely necessary.

Consult your physician concerning any medication that you carry and inquire about potential complications or side effects. Make sure you are not allergic to any drugs that you intend to use. Sharing medications with others is potentially dangerous and is not recommended.

Remember, the value of any first-aid book or medical kit is both enhanced and limited by the ability of the owner to use the information and contents effectively and creatively.

Taking a course in Wilderness First Aid, Wilderness First Responder or Emergency Medical Technician, and practicing your skills before you leave home, will better prepare you to manage an emergency when it occurs.

The author and publisher disclaim any liability for injuries, disability or death that may result from the use of the information in this book, correct or otherwise, or the products in any Adventure Medical kit.

May all of your journeys be safe, healthy, and filled with adventure!

CONTENTS

INTRODUCTION

At the heart of wilderness medicine is improvisation, a unique amalgam of medical science integrated with creativity and ingenuity. In the wilderness, one must utilize whatever supplies or materials are on hand and depend heavily on common sense. Throughout the text you will find boxes with information titled **"Weiss Advice,"** which describe improvised wilderness medicine techniques. Most of these recommendations are supported by research published in medical journals. However, some are merely anecdotal, based on my own personal experience and training.

'WEISS ADVICE'

[IMPROVISED TECHNIQUE]

Another common feature is **"When to Worry,"** boxes intended to help the reader identify situations in which immediate evacuation from the wilderness is recommended. They are only general guidelines, however, and ultimately the circumstance, combined with your own resources, training, and experience should dictate your actions. When in doubt, it is always better to get out and seek help rather than wait and see what happens.

WHEN TO WORRY

WHERE TO BEGIN:
THE THREE ABCS OF WILDERNESS FIRST AID

There are six immediate priorities in wilderness first aid, regardless of the injury or illness. The acronym, "THREE ABCs," is a helpful mantra for recalling the six priorities. This expanded primary survey is a rapid evaluation of the scene and the patient in which life-threatening conditions, such as a blocked airway, severe bleeding, and cardiac arrest are recognized and simultaneous management is begun.

THE THREE ABCs

A1	**ASSESS** the scene
A2	**AIRWAY** (ensure an open airway)
A3	**ALERT** others
B1	**BARRIERS** (gloves, pocket mask)
B2	**BREATHING** (check for breathing and perform rescue breathing if necessary)
B3	**BLEEDING**
C1	**CPR** (start CPR if the victim has no pulse)
C2	**CERVICAL SPINE** (prevent unnecessary movement of the head and neck)
C3	**COVER** and protect the victim from the environment

A1: ASSESS THE SCENE

Always ensure the safety of the uninjured members of the party first. Assess the scene for further hazards, such as rockfall, avalanche, or dangerous animals before rendering any first aid. The worst thing you can do is create another victim or become one yourself. Avoid approaching the victim from directly above if there is a possibility of a rock or snow slide. Do not allow your sense of urgency to transform an accident into a risky and foolish rescue attempt.

A2: AIRWAY

Speak loudly to the victim as you approach. A response indicates that he is breathing and has a pulse. For infants and children, gently tap them on their hands and feet and call their name. If the victim is unresponsive, immediately determine if he is breathing.

If he is face down, roll him onto his back so that the head, shoulders and torso move as a single unit without twisting (**Fig. 1**). Place your ear and cheek close to the victim's mouth and nose to detect air movement, while looking for movement of the chest and abdomen (**Fig. 2**). In cold weather, look for a vapor cloud and feel for warm air movement.

Fig. 1 - Log-rolling a victim face-up without twisting the spine.

If the victim is not breathing, clean the mouth out with your fingers and open the airway. If you do not suspect trauma, the airway can be opened by placing the palm of one hand on the forehead and tilting the head back while the fingers of the other hand lift the chin

Fig. 2 - Check for breathing.

(Fig. 3). The most common
reason for an airway obstruction in an unconscious victim is
relaxation of the muscles of the
tongue and throat, which allows
the tongue to fall back and block
the airway.

Fig. 3 - *Opening the airway of an
unconscious victim when trauma
is not suspected.*

'WEISS ADVICE'

[IMPROVISED TECHNIQUE]

Opening the airway with two safety pins

Keeping the airway open with the jaw thrust technique ties up your hands. If you are by yourself, an airway can be kept open by pinning the front of the victim's tongue to his lower lip with two safety pins. An alternative to pinning the lower lip is to pass a string or shoelace through the pin in the tongue and keep it forward by tying it to the victim's shirt button or jacket zipper.

It sounds barbaric, but this technique pulls the tongue forward and prevents it from obstructing the airway. Any victim who requires this life-saving maneuver will not mind the small holes, and will, of course, not notice the discomfort. It also frees up your hands for other tasks.

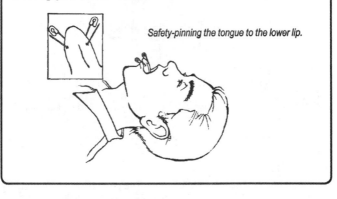

Safety-pinning the tongue to the lower lip.

A3:   ALERT OTHERS

Before becoming more involved with the resuscitation, take a few seconds to call or send someone for help and to alert others to the accident.

B1:   BARRIERS
Any time you deal with blood or bodily fluids, it is vitally important to protect yourself from blood-borne germs, such as hepatitis and the AIDS virus. One out of every 300 people in the United States is now infected with the HIV virus, and the risk of infectious hepatitis is far greater. Protect your hands with virus-proof gloves and use a barrier device when performing mouth-to-mouth rescue breathing. Even latex gloves can leak, so make sure you wash your hands or wipe them with an antimicrobial towelette after removing the gloves.

WARNING: Five to seven percent of the population and more than 10 percent of all medical personnel are allergic to latex. Latex allergies can produce skin rashes, severe anaphylactic reactions and death. If you suspect that you might have an allergy to latex, use powder-free Nitrile gloves.

'WEISS ADVICE'
[IMPROVISED TECHNIQUE]

Improvised Barrier
Any gloves are better than using your bare hands. Dishwashing gloves make an effective barrier to blood. An improvised glove can also be made by placing your hand inside a sandwich or garbage bag and securing it to your wrist with tape or string.

B2:   BREATHING
If the patient does not breathe on his own after establishing an airway, then begin mouth-to-mouth rescue breathing (See page 12).

'WEISS ADVICE'

[IMPROVISED TECHNIQUE]

Improvised barrier for mouth-to-mouth breathing

A glove can be modified and used as a barrier shield for performing rescue breathing. Simply cut the middle finger of the glove at its halfway point and insert it into the victim's mouth. Stretch the glove across the victim's mouth and blow into the glove as you would to inflate a balloon. The slit creates a one-way valve, preventing backflow of the victim's saliva.

Improvised glove barrier.

B3:   BLEEDING

Check the victim for signs of profuse bleeding. Feel inside any bulky clothing and check underneath the victim. To stop bleeding, use your gloved hand to apply pressure directly to the wound. If bleeding from an extremity cannot be stopped by direct pressure and the victim is in danger of bleeding to death, apply a tourniquet. A tourniquet is any band applied around an arm or leg so tightly that all blood flow beyond the band is cut off. If the tourniquet is left on for more than four hours, the arm or leg beyond the tourniquet may die and require amputation. Damage to the arm or leg is rare if the tourniquet is left on less than two hours.

In the face of massive extremity hemorrhage, it is better to accept the small risk of damage to the limb than to have a victim bleed to death.

How to Apply a Tourniquet

1. Tourniquet material should be wide and flat, to prevent crushing tissue. Use a firm bandage, belt or strap that is three to four inches wide and that will not stretch. Never use wire, rope or any material that will cut the skin.
2. Wrap the bandage snugly around the extremity several times as close above the wound as possible, and tie an overhand knot.
3. Place a stick or similar object on the knot and tie another overhand knot over the stick.
4. Twist the stick until the bandage becomes tight enough to stop the bleeding. Tie or tape the stick in place to prevent it from unraveling.
5. Mark the victim with a TK, and note the time the tourniquet was applied.
6. If you are more than an hour from medical care, loosen the tourniquet very slowly at the end of one hour, while maintaining direct pressure on the wound. If bleeding is still heavy, retighten the tourniquet. If bleeding is now manageable with direct pressure alone, leave the tourniquet in place, but do not tighten it again unless severe bleeding starts.

Applying a tourniquet.

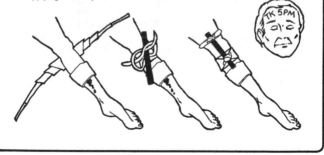

C1:   CPR

Place your index and middle finger on the victim's throat over the Adam's apple and then slide your fingers down the side of the victim's neck to the space between the Adam's apple and neck muscle to feel the carotid pulse **(Fig. 8)**. Hold your fingers here for at least 30 seconds (60 seconds if the victim is cold or hypothermic) and feel for any pulsation. If you do not detect a pulse, combine chest compression with mouth-to-mouth rescue breathing (See page 12).

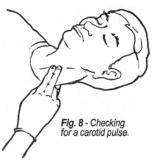

Fig. 8 - Checking for a carotid pulse.

C2:   CERVICAL SPINE

The spinal cord is vital for life and runs down through the vertebrae in the neck. Spinal cord damage can cause permanent paralysis or death. It is necessary to immobilize the head, neck and torso after an accident which could have broken the victim's neck, such as a fall, head injury, or diving injury, and if any of the following are present:
- The victim is unconscious;
- The victim complains of neck or back pain;
- There is tenderness in the back of the neck or upper back when touched;
- There is numbness, tingling, or altered sensation in the extremities;
- The victim is unable to move or has weakness in an arm or leg not due to direct trauma to that part;
- The victim has an altered level of consciousness, or is under the influence of drugs or alcohol;
- The victim has another very painful injury that may distract him from the pain in his neck, such as a thigh (femur) or pelvis fracture, dislocated shoulder, or broken rib.

If a cervical spine injury is suspected, the rescuer should immobilize the victim's head and neck and prevent any movement of his torso (See page 63). Avoid moving the victim with a suspected spine injury if he is in a safe location. The victim should be evacuated by professional rescuers.

C3:   COVER AND PROTECT THE VICTIM

If it is cold, place insulating garments or blankets underneath and on top of the victim to protect him from hypothermia. Remove and replace any wet clothing. If it is hot, loosen the victim's clothing and create shade. If the victim is in a dangerous area, move him to a safer location while maintaining spine immobilization if indicated.

WHAT TO DO NEXT: THE SECONDARY SURVEY

Once you have completed the primary survey and made sure that there are no life-threatening problems, perform a head-to-toe examination of the victim, looking for further evidence of injury. Look at, and gently push on every part of the victim, looking for swelling, pain, or deformity.

Definition of Signs and Symptoms

Diagnosis of an injury or illness relies on the ability of the rescuer to examine the victim thoroughly and identify important medical clues called signs and symptoms.

Signs are the things you observe when you examine a victim with your eyes, ears, nose and hands. For example, you might see bluish discoloration of the skin, hear labored or noisy breathing, smell pus in a wound infection, or feel swelling under the skin.

Symptoms are what the victim tells you he is experiencing, such as pain, nausea, dizziness, or headache.

ORGANIZE A RESCUE TEAM

In the wilderness, developing a team approach at the site of the accident is vital to the success of the rescue. Begin by designating a leader. This individual can be the climb leader, head boatman, or anyone who assumes the role. This person should direct all first-aid efforts and delegate duties, rather than perform them, when possible. If the leader becomes intimately involved in a specific function, he loses the ability to maintain a team effort. The leader should evaluate the victim's injuries, party size, and terrain, and develop a plan for either evacuating the patient or obtaining professional assistance.

LIFE THREATENING EMERGENCIES
(RESCUE BREATHING/CPR/CHOKING)

RESCUE BREATHING

Rescue Breathing: Adults

1) Check for breathing (See page 3). If the victim is not lying on his back, gently roll him over, moving the entire body as a unit while maintaining spine precautions.

2) If no breathing is detected, open the airway with the head-tilt maneuver. Place the palm of one hand on the forehead and tilt the head back while the fingers of the other hand grasp and lift the chin (**Fig. 9**). Sweep two fingers through the victim's mouth to remove any foreign material or broken teeth.

Fig. 9 - Opening the airway.

3) If the victim does not start to breathe on his own, pinch his nostrils closed and place your mouth over his mouth (**Fig. 11**). A CPR barrier or modified glove (see page 7) can be used during mouth-to-mouth rescue breathing to prevent physical contact with the victim's mouth.

4) Blow air into the victim until you see the chest rise. Remove your mouth to allow the victim to exhale. Give two initial breaths.

5) Repeat this procedure, giving a vigorous breath every five to six seconds until the victim starts to breathe spontaneously, help arrives, or you are too exhausted to continue.

6) If air does not move in and out of the victim's mouth easily or if the chest does not rise, perform another head tilt-chin lift before attempting the second breath. If breathing still does not occur, the airway may be obstructed by a foreign

body (See Choking: obstructed airway).

7) During mouth-to-mouth rescue breathing, the victim's stomach will often fill with air, eventually resulting in vomiting. If vomiting occurs, log-roll the victim in a manner that maintains spine alignment, and clear the airway **(Fig. 12 a-b)**.

Fig. 11 - Rescue breathing, adult.

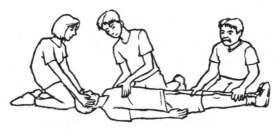

Fig. 12a - Log-rolling the victim with multiple rescuers.

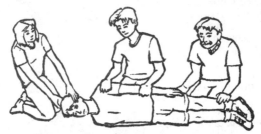

Fig. 12b - Log-rolling the victim with multiple rescuers.

8) Check for a pulse by feeling for the carotid artery in the victim's neck for 10 seconds (**Fig. 13**). If the victim is hypothermic, feel for one full minute before deciding that he has no pulse. If a pulse is present, continue rescue breathing. If no pulse is present, start chest compression.

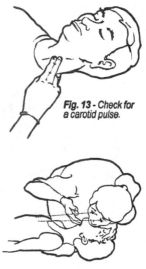

Fig. 13 - Check for a carotid pulse.

Rescue Breathing: Child (older than one year)

1) Cover the child's mouth with your mouth. Pinch the child's nose closed with the thumb and forefinger of your hand that is on the forehead for the head tilt. Use your other hand to lift the chin (**Fig. 14**).

2) Breathe two breaths at 1 second/breath into the child's mouth. You should breathe enough air in to make the child's chest rise.

3) If the child does not start to breathe on his own, check for a pulse. If a pulse is present, continue rescue breathing with a

Fig. 14 - Rescue breathing, child.

breath every 3 to 5 seconds. If no pulse is present, start chest compression.

CARDIOPULMONARY RESUSCITATION (CPR)

CPR is the combination of rescue (mouth-to-mouth) breathing and chest compression in a pulseless and non-breathing victim.

When to Start and Stop CPR

Do not be afraid to start CPR, fearing that you might be criticized for not continuing it indefinitely. There is an old saying in medicine that, "once started, CPR should never be stopped in the field." To adhere to this dictum is not only impractical, it is potentially hazardous to the rescuers and has no place in modern wilderness medicine. It is well established that after 10 to 15 minutes of CPR, victims who do not respond never will. The only rare exceptions have been victims who were profoundly hypothermic. It may be better to give the victim the benefit of the doubt and start CPR, even if he has been without a heartbeat or breath for a prolonged time. It is difficult to know exactly how long a person found unconscious has actually been in cardiac arrest.

If CPR is not successful in resuscitating the victim after 15 to 30 minutes, and the victim is not profoundly hypothermic, you can discontinue the effort.

CHEST COMPRESSION: ADULT

1) Place the victim on his back on a firm surface. Position the heel of one hand over the center of the victim's breastbone, two fingers up from his xyphoid, and the heel of your second hand over the bottom hand, interlocking the fingers **(Fig. 15)**.

2) Your shoulders should line up directly over the victim's breastbone, with elbows straight.

3) Keeping your arms stiff and using a smooth motion, compress the breastbone 1-1/2 to 2 inches, then release. The compression phase should equal the relaxation phase, with a rate of 100 compressions per minute (count out loud, "one-and-two-and-three-and..."). Do not remove your hands from the victim's chest between compressions **(Fig. 16)**.

4) If two rescuers are working together, the first rescuer should pause after every thirty compressions so the second rescuer can give the victim two breaths. If a single person is performing the rescue, he should alternate 30 chest compressions with two breaths.

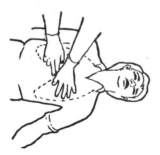

Fig. 15 - CPR hand placement, adult.

Fig. 16 - CPR hand position, adult.

CHEST COMPRESSION:
CHILD (OLDER THAN ONE YEAR)

1) Place the heel of your hand on the child's lower breast-bone, with your fingers lifted off the chest (**Fig. 17**).

2) Compress the breastbone about one-third to one-half the thickness of the chest (1 to 1-1/2 inches).

3) Compress the chest at a rate of approximately 100 per minute, stopping to give the child two breaths every thirty compressions.

4) Continue the compression-to-breathing ratio of thirty to two.

Use this same ratio whether one or two people are doing the resuscitation. Continue until an AED arrives, the victim begins to move, or professional responders take over.

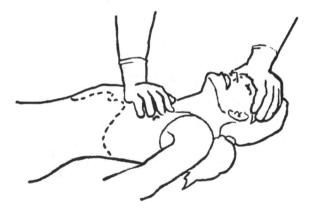

Fig. 17 - CPR hand placement, child.

CHOKING/OBSTRUCTED AIRWAY

Choking is a life-threatening emergency that occurs when something blocks the victim's airway so that he cannot breathe. Choking should be suspected when an individual suddenly becomes agitated and clutches his throat, especially while eating. The victim may be unable to speak and then become cyanotic (turn blue).

Choking Adult & Child (Heimlich Maneuver)

1) Stand behind the victim and wrap your arms around the victim's waist. Make a fist with one of your hands and place it just above the victim's navel and below the rib cage, with the thumb side against his abdomen.

2) Grasp your fist with your other hand and pull it forcefully toward you, into the victim's abdomen and slightly upward with a quick thrust. If unsuccessful, repeat the procedure **(Fig. 18)**.

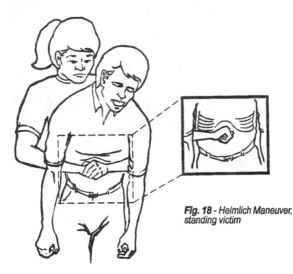

Fig. 18 - Heimlich Maneuver, standing victim

If the adult or child becomes unconscious:

1) Lay the victim on his back and attempt rescue breathing (See page 12).

2) If you cannot get air into the victim and/or the chest does not rise with rescue breathing, perform the Heimlich maneuver while kneeling and straddling the victim's thighs. Use the heel of your hand instead of your fist (**Fig. 19**).

3) If still unsuccessful, sweep the mouth with one or two fingers to try to remove any foreign material. Continue to perform the Heimlich maneuver and periodically attempt rescue breathing. If multiple attempts at clearing the airway and breathing air into the patient are unsuccessful, a cricothyrodotomy (surgical airway) is indicated.

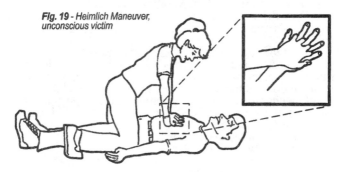

Fig. 19 - Heimlich Maneuver, unconscious victim

CRICOTHYRODOTOMY (SURGICAL AIRWAY)

A cricothyrodotomy is a technique which allows rapid entrance to the air passage in a victim who is unable to breathe from a blocked airway. It is a very challenging and potentially complication-prone procedure, but one that may be lifesaving. It should be attempted only after the Heimlich and other non-invasive airway techniques to relieve the obstruction in the airway have been exhausted, and the victim is on the verge of dying from lack of air.

In the wilderness, a cricothyrodotomy is done by cutting a hole in the thin cricothyroid membrane of the windpipe (trachea) and by placing a hollow object into the trachea to let air enter into the lungs. The cricothyroid membrane lies just below the Adam's apple in the center of the neck, and feels like a small depression between the Adam's apple and the firm ring below it called the cricoid cartilage.

How to Perform a Cricothyrodotomy

1) With the victim lying on his back, clean the neck around the Adam's apple with an antiseptic if one is readily available. Put on protective gloves.

2) Find the Adam's apple with your finger (this is the most prominent firm structure in the center of the neck). Slowly run your finger downward toward the chest (keep your finger in the midline of the neck as you do this) until you feel a small indentation between the bottom of the Adam's apple and the top of the cricoid cartilage (the next firm and prominent structure that you feel as you move down the neck). The indentation between the Adam's apple and the cricoid cartilage in the windpipe is called the cricothyroid membrane and is the spot that you want to puncture **(Fig. 20)**.

3) Make a vertical one-inch incision through the skin with a knife over the membrane (go a little bit above and below the membrane) while using the

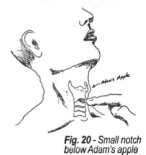

Fig. 20 - Small notch below Adam's apple

fingers of your other hand to pry the skin edges apart. Anticipate bleeding from the wound. After the skin is cut apart, puncture the membrane by stabbing it with your knife or other pointy object **(Fig. 21)**.

Fig. 21 - Making a one-inch incision through the skin

4) Stabilizing the windpipe between the fingers of one hand, insert a hollow object such as the barrel of a syringe (see below) or ball point pen casing or stiff straw through the membrane with your other hand. Secure the object in place with tape.

5) Breathe air into the victim through the object, as if you were blowing through a straw, and then remover your mouth to allow exhaled air to exit. Repeat this step at the same frequently as if you were performing mouth-to-mouth rescue breathing.

Using a syringe as a breathing tube (Fig. 22-23)

Remove the plunger from the barrel of a 3 cc or 1 cc syringe. Using a sharp knife or saw, cut the barrel at a 45-degree angle at its midpoint to create an improvised airway for inserting through the cricothyroid membrane.

Fig. 22 - Cutting the barrel of a 3 cc or 1 cc syringe

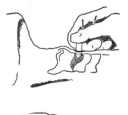

Fig. 23 - Inserting a hollow object through the membrane

SHOCK

Shock is a life-threatening condition in which blood flow to the tissues of the body is inadequate and cells are deprived of oxygen. Any serious injury or illness can produce shock. Examples are severe bleeding (either external or internal), thigh (femur) or pelvis fractures, major burns, dehydration, heart failure, severe allergic reactions, or spinal cord injuries with paralysis.

Signs and Symptoms

The skin may be pale, cool, or clammy. The pulse is weak and rapid or even undetectable (in shock produced by a spinal cord injury, the pulse will remain normal or slow). Breathing may be shallow, rapid, or irregular. Mental status may be altered (the victim may be confused, restless, or combative).

Treatment:

It is important to recognize shock and to transport the victim to a medical facility immediately.

1) Keep the victim lying down, covered and warm. Remember to insulate him from the ground as well.
2) Stop any obvious signs of bleeding.
3) Loosen any restrictive clothing.
4) Splint all broken bones. If the femur bone is fractured, apply and maintain traction (See page 76). If a pelvic fracture is suspected, apply a pelvic wrap (See page 70).
5) Elevate the legs so that gravity can help improve the blood supply to the heart and brain only if the victim has shock from external bleeding which has been controlled, or has fainted. If the victim has internal bleeding, avoid unnecessary movement and keep him lying flat. For heart failure shock, the victim may be more comfortable with his head and shoulders raised slightly.

HEAD INJURIES

Head trauma and brain injury can result from direct impact or from the shearing forces produced by rapid deceleration. When your head hits a hard object such as a boulder, the impact can fracture the skull, bruise the brain, or cause severe bleeding inside the brain from damaged blood vessels. Shearing forces from sudden deceleration of the brain against the inside of the skull can also tear blood vessels on the surface of the brain, leading to an expanding blood clot and pressure on the brain (intracranial pressure).

Rising intracranial pressure is bad for several reasons. The increased pressure makes it difficult for the heart to pump enough blood to the head. This is a major catastrophe for the brain, which depends on a constant supply of blood to bring it oxygen and other nutrients. If the pressure within the skull rises high enough, it can force parts of the brain downward through the base of the skull (herniation), causing damage to the brain structures and, ultimately, death. Compression of one of the nerves as the brain swells produces dilatation of one or both pupils, an important sign of a severe head injury.

Head Injuries Can Be Subdivided Into Three Groups:
  1) Prolonged unconsciousness (more than five to 10 minutes);
  2) Brief loss of consciousness;
  3) No loss of consciousness.

PROLONGED UNCONSCIOUSNESS

Loss of consciousness for more than five to 10 minutes is a sign of significant brain injury. Assess the victim's airway and perform rescue breathing if necessary. Because there is a potential for accompanying neck and spine injuries with severe head trauma, the victim's spine should be immobilized. Immediately evacuate the victim to a medical facility. During transportation, maintain spine immobilization and keep the victim's head pointed uphill on sloping terrain. Be prepared to log-roll the victim onto his side if he vomits. Continually monitor his airway for signs of obstruction (listen for noisy or labored breathing) and a decreasing respiratory rate.

BRIEF LOSS OF CONSCIOUSNESS

Short-term unconsciousness, in which the victim wakes after a minute or two and gradually regains normal mental status and physical abilities, is evidence of a concussion. A concussion does not usually produce permanent damage, although confusion or amnesia about the event and repetitive questioning by the victim are common.

To be safe, evacuate the victim to a medical facility for evaluation. At a minimum in the backcountry, you should keep the victim under close observation for at least 24 hours, and not allow him to perform potentially hazardous activities. Normal sleep should be interrupted every three to four hours to check briefly that the victim's condition has not deteriorated and that he can be easily aroused. If the victim becomes increasingly lethargic, confused or combative, is just not acting his normal self, or if he develops any of the other signs on the head injury checklist (see below), he should be evacuated to a medical center immediately.

NO LOSS OF CONSCIOUSNESS

If an individual hits his head but never loses consciousness, it's rarely serious. He may have a mild headache, may bleed from a scalp wound, or a have a large bump on his head, but evacuation isn't necessary unless he develops any of the problems listed on the head injury checklist.

HEAD INJURY CHECKLIST

Seek immediate medical attention if any of the following symptoms occur after a blow to the head:
- Headache that progressively worsens;
- Consciousness gradually deteriorates from alertness to drowsiness or disorientation; Ask the victim if he knows his name, location, the date, and what happened. If he gets all four correct, he is oriented X 4.
- Persistent or projectile (shoots out under pressure) vomiting;
- One pupil becomes significantly larger than the other;
- Bleeding from an ear or nose without direct injury to those areas, or a clear watery fluid draining from the nose;
- Bruising behind the ears or around the eyes, when there is no direct injury to those areas;
- Seizures.

SKULL FRACTURES

Fracture of the skull is not life threatening unless associated with underlying brain injury or severe bleeding.

Signs of a skull fracture include a sensation that the skull is uneven when touching the scalp, blood or clear fluid draining from the ears or nose without direct trauma to those areas, and black and blue discoloration around the eyes (raccoon eyes) or behind the ears (Battle's sign).

Treatment:
Evacuate the victim to a medical facility as soon as possible.

SCALP WOUNDS

Scalp lacerations are common after head injuries, and tend to bleed a lot because of their rich blood supply. Fortunately, bleeding can usually be stopped by applying direct pressure to the wound with your gloved hand. It might be necessary to hold pressure for up to 30 minutes.

'WEISS ADVICE'
[IMPROVISED TECHNIQUE]

Hair-tying a scalp wound closed

If you're faced with a bleeding scalp wound and the injured person has a healthy head of hair, you can tie the wound closed using the victim's own hair. Take a piece of heavy silk suture material (dental floss works well) and lay it on top of, and parallel to the wound. Twirl a few strands of hair on opposite sides of the wound and pull them together tightly, forcing the wound edges closed. Use the suture material to tie the opposing strands of hair together with a square knot.

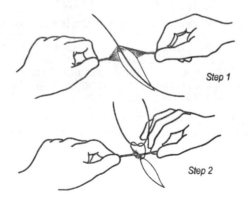

Step 1

Step 2

HEADACHE

At least 60 percent of the population will have a significant headache at some time in their lives, and it is one of the most common reasons for visiting a physician. Headaches can stem from innumerable causes, including tension and stress, migraine, dehydration, altitude illness (see page 137), alcohol hangover, carbon monoxide poisoning, brain tumors, strokes, aneurysms, intracranial bleeds, fever, flu, meningitis and other infectious diseases, high blood pressure, sinus infections (page 102), and dental problems (page 36). Suddenly going "cold turkey" on caffeine during a backpacking trip, especially if you regularly drink more than three cups of coffee a day, can also precipitate a headache.

TENSION HEADACHE
(Stress or Muscle Contraction Headache)
This is the most common type of headache and affects people of all ages. Pain is related to continuous contractions of the muscles of the head and neck and can last from 30 minutes to seven days. The headache is often described as tight or viselike, and felt on both sides, especially in the back of the head and neck. The pain is not made worse by walking, climbing or performing physical activity.
Sensitivity to light may occur, but nausea and vomiting are not usually present.

Treatment
Loosen any tight fitting pack straps or hat, and adjust your pack so that it rides comfortably. Ibuprofen (Motrin®) 600 mg or acetaminophen (Tylenol®) 1,000 mg may help relieve the discomfort. A neck and scalp massage from your partner may be beneficial.

MIGRAINE HEADACHE
The term migraine is often used as a catch-all phrase but should be reserved for those headaches that show specific patterns. These are recurrent headaches that usually start during adolescence and typically involve only one side of the head (they can be also be experienced on both sides of the head) and are associated with nausea, vomiting and sensitivity to light. Walking or physical exertion make the pain worse.

About 15 percent of people with migraine headaches will experience an aura (flashing lights, distorted shapes and colors, blurred vision or other visual apparitions) prior to the onset of the headache.

Treatment

Ibuprofen (Motrin®) 800 mg along with caffeinated beverages such as coffee may help relieve symptoms, especially if taken early. Stronger prescription medications such as Tylenol with codeine, Vicodin® and Imitrex® or Relpax® may be needed. Lying down in the shade with a cool compress on the forehead may be helpful.

DEHYDRATION HEADACHE

Headache can be an early sign of dehydration. The pain is felt on both sides of the head and is usually made worse when the victim stands from a lying position.

Treatment

Resting and drinking at least one to two quarts of water should relieve the pain. On average, you need to drink about four quarts a day when backpacking. A good barometer of your hydration status is the color of your urine. If it is not clear like gin, then you're not drinking enough.

SINUS HEADACHE

Sinus headache is usually associated with a sinus infection and typified by fever, nasal congestion, production of nasal discharge, and pain in the front of the face. Tapping over the sinuses may increase the pain.

Treatment

Use an oral decongestant (pseudoephedrine), nasal spray (Neo-Synephrine or Afrin), and an antibiotic (amoxicillin (Augmentin®), azithromycin (Zithromax®), or erythromycin).

MENINGITIS

This is a severe infection that involves the lining of the brain and spinal cord. The headache of meningitis is severe and often accompanied by nausea, vomiting, fever, altered level of consciousness (confusion or bizarre behavior are examples), and a stiff neck. The victim may demonstrate discomfort when the chin is flexed downward against the chest, and may complain that the pain also occurs in the back. An infant can suffer meningitis without a stiff neck and may manifest only poor feeding, fever, lethargy and irritability.

Treatment

If meningitis is suspected, the victim should be started on broad-spectrum antibiotics and evacuated immediately.

WHEN TO WORRY

HEADACHES

Some headaches may signal a life-threatening illness. Get to a medical facility as soon as possible if you experience any of the following:

1) The headache is the worst of your life and came on suddenly and severely (aneurysms or intracranial bleeding).

2) Your arms and legs on one side are weak, numb or paralyzed, or one side of your face appears droopy (stroke).

3) You are unable to talk or express yourself clearly (stroke).

4) You have a fever, stiff neck or any rash (meningitis).

5) Your headache grows steadily worse over time (brain tumor).

6) You have repetitive vomiting.

7) Seizures or convulsions develop.

8) The pain does not go away over a period of 24 hours.

EYE PROBLEMS

EYE TRAUMA

If the eye is hit, a visible layer of blood may settle behind the cornea during the next six to eight hours. In this case, the eye should be patched closed with a gauze pad and tape. Transport the victim immediately to medical care, keeping the head elevated and in an upright position.

If the eyeball is perforated, the victim will experience a loss of vision ranging from blurred sight to total blindness. Other signs and symptoms include pain, a dilated and unreactive pupil and blood in the eye. Do not rinse the eye or try to remove any object stuck into the eyeball. Cover the eye with a paper cone, cup, or other protective object and secure this protective covering in place with a bandage. Be careful not to put pressure on the eye. If possible, patch both eyes or have the victim keep both eyes closed. Evacuate the victim to a medical facility immediately. If evacuation will be delayed more than six hours, start antibiotic therapy with penicillin, Keflex® or erythromycin.

Trauma to the eye can also cause the retina to become detached from the back of the eye. Symptoms include persistent light flashes and floating spots in the field of vision. Vision loss is painless. A detached retina requires surgical repair. Seek immediate medical care.

'WEISS ADVICE'

[IMPROVISED TECHNIQUE]

Relieving eye pain

Drops of tea squeezed from a cool, non-herbal tea bag may help to soothe the eye and relieve pain.

SCRATCHED EYE (Corneal Abrasion)

The clear covering over the front of the eye, called the cornea, is easily scratched or abraded.

Signs and Symptoms

1) The victim will feel as if he has sand in his eye.
2) The eye will usually appear bloodshot, and there is often tearing and slight blurring of vision.
3) Intense pain, made worse by blinking the eyes, may occur, and there is sensitivity to light.
4) Close inspection of the cornea may show a slight irregularity on its surface.

Treatment

1) Check the eyes carefully for foreign material, making sure to examine under the upper lid.
2) Cool compresses may help relieve some of the irritation.
3) If available, apply antibiotic drops such as Tobrex® every two to three hours while awake for two to three days.
4) Administer pain medication to the victim and have him rest his eyes as much as possible. Most of the time, the injury heals by itself in one to two days.
5) Patching the eye with an eye patch or a bandage for 24 hours may help to reduce pain. If an eye patch or other bandage is not available, the eye can be taped closed or the victim can wear sunglasses. An eye should not be patched closed if there is any sign of infection.

WHEN TO WORRY

Scratched Eye

Seek medical care immediately if the victim has a scratched eye or snow blindness and any of the following signs or symptoms occur: The injury does not heal spontaneously in two days; there is increasing redness, pain or swelling; greenish fluid begins to drain from the eye; or the victim's vision worsens.

SNOW BLINDNESS

Snow blindness is a sunburn to the eye from intense ultraviolet radiation at high altitude or while traveling in the snow which results in a corneal abrasion. Unfortunately, you are unaware that the injury is occurring until it is too late, because signs and symptoms of snow blindness are delayed by about six hours from the time of exposure to the light. Wearing adequate eye protection (100% UV blocking sunglasses with side protectors) can prevent snow blindness.

Signs, Symptoms and Treatment are the same as for a scratched eye (see above).

'WEISS ADVICE'

[IMPROVISED TECHNIQUE]

Improvised Sunglasses

If you forget or lose your sunglasses, you can cut slits in a piece of cardboard, such as one side of a cracker or cereal box, or a piece of duct tape folded back over onto itself. These should be just wide enough to see through. Tape or tie this around your head to minimize the amount of ultraviolet light hitting your eyes.

SUBCONJUNCTIVAL HEMORRHAGE

Small blood clots on the white part of the eye sometimes occur after physical exertion, coughing or strangulation. This is not a serious condition. The hemorrhage will resorb over a few weeks.

SUPERFICIAL FOREIGN BODIES

If a foreign body enters the eye but is not imbedded into the eyeball, attempt to remove it by irrigating the eye with a stream of water.

If irrigation does not remove the foreign body, carefully and gently attempt to lift the material out with a moistened cotton swab or cloth. Sometimes the foreign body will lodge underneath the upper eyelid. If this occurs, the upper eyelid should be firmly grasped by the eyelashes while the victim looks downward. Fold it inside out over a cotton swab. The object can then be removed with the corner of a moistened cloth or another cotton swab.

[IMPROVISED TECHNIQUE]

Eye Irrigation
  Pour disinfected water into a sandwich or garbage bag and puncture the bottom of the bag with a safety pin. Squeeze the top of the bag firmly to create an irrigation stream, which can then be directed into the eye.

After objects are removed from the eye, victims often report feeling as if something is still in their eye. This is usually caused by small scratches on the surface of the cornea. Treat the same as for a scratched eye (see above).

INFECTIONS
  Eye infections are characterized by red, itchy eye(s) with yellow or green discharge, crusted eyelashes, and swollen lids.

Treatment
  Irrigate the eye with water. Antibiotic eye drops can be prescribed by a physician. Tobrex® drops applied to the eye every two to three hours while awake is my usual choice.

STYES OR ABSCESSES
  Styes or abscesses on the eyelid produce localized swelling, redness, and pain.

Treatment
  When a sty begins to develop, apply warm, moist compresses to the eyelid for 30 minutes four times a day, until the sty either disappears, or enlarges and comes to a head. If it comes to a head but does not drain spontaneously, seek medical attention. If the victim is more than 48 hours from medical care and the infection is progressing to include the cheek or forehead, the sty may be carefully lanced with a scalpel or pin. This should be followed by antibiotic therapy, including dicloxacillin, erythromycin, or cephalexin (Keflex®).

NOSEBLEEDS

Nosebleeds usually can be controlled by pinching the soft part of the nostrils together between your fingers and holding firmly for at least 15 to 20 minutes. If blood continues to drain down the back of the throat despite pinching the nostrils tightly, it indicates a posterior (back of the nose) bleed. This is a serious problem, as the victim can lose a significant amount of blood. If the bleeding does not stop on its own after a few minutes, you may need to pack both the back and front of the nose (see below). If the bleeding stops when you pinch the nostrils, but resumes when you let go after 20 minutes of firm pressure, you may need to pack only the front of the nose (see below).

'WEISS ADVICE'
[IMPROVISED TECHNIQUE]

Packing the front of the nose

Packing the front of the nose in the backcountry
If bleeding cannot be controlled by pinching the nostrils together for a full 20 minutes, nasal packing should be considered. If available, first insert a piece of cotton or gauze soaked with a blood vessel constrictor such as Afrin® or Neo-Synephrine® nasal spray into the nose, leave it in place for five minutes, and then remove it. Cut a large gauze pad or soft cotton cloth into a thin continuous strip and coat this with petroleum jelly or antibiotic ointment. Gently pack it into the nostril, using tweezers or a thin twig so that both ends of the packing material remain outside of the nasal cavity (start the packing with the middle of the strip). This will keep the packing from going down the back of the throat. To completely pack the nasal cavity of an adult, about three feet of packing is required. Leave the pack in for 24 to 48 hours, and then gently remove it. If bleeding starts again, repack the nostril.

Packing the nose will block sinus drainage and predispose the victim to a sinus infection. Antibiotics such as Septra®, Augmentin®, Keflex® or amoxicillin should be taken until the packing is removed.

Packing the back of the nose in the backcountry

Bleeding from the back of the nose can be difficult to control, and requires a posterior pack. A 14-to-16 french Foley catheter (something you may want to add to your first aid kit) can be used to pack the back of the nose. First lubricate the catheter with either petroleum jelly or antibiotic ointment, and then insert it through the nasal cavity to the back of the throat. If the victim's mouth is open, you should be able to see the tip of the catheter in the throat behind the tongue. Inflate the balloon of the catheter with 10 to 15 ml of air from a syringe and gently draw the catheter back out of the nose until resistance is met. Secure the catheter firmly to the victim's forehead with several strips of tape. The front of the nose should then be packed as described earlier.

DENTAL EMERGENCIES

TOOTHACHE

The common toothache is caused by inflammation of the dental pulp and is often associated with a cavity. The pain may be severe and intermittent and is made worse by hot or cold foods or liquids.

Treatment

1) If the offending cavity can be localized, a piece of cotton soaked with a topical anti-inflammatory agent such as eugenol (oil of cloves) can first be applied.
2) Place a temporary filling material, such as Cavit® or zinc-oxide and eugenol cement, into the cavity or lost

---

'WEISS ADVICE'

[IMPROVISED TECHNIQUE]

Replacing a lost filling

Melt some candle wax and allow it to cool until it is just soft and pliable. Place the wax into the cavity or lost filling site and smooth it out with your finger. Have the victim bite down to seat the wax in place and remove any excess wax.

---

filling site to protect the nerve.

DENTAL INFECTIONS AND ABSCESSES

Dental pain associated with swelling in the gum line at the base of the tooth might indicate a tooth infection or abscess. Tapping the offending tooth causes pain, but the tooth should not be sensitive to hot or cold. Dental infections occasionally spread beyond the tooth to the floor of the mouth, face and neck. If this occurs, the victim may have difficulty opening his mouth, swallowing or breathing, and fever and swelling of the face may develop.

Treatment
Make every effort to locate a dentist, as this can lead to serious illness and often requires intravenous antibiotics, as well as extraction of the tooth or root canal therapy. Swelling of the face indicates a much more severe infection and can lead to a life-threatening condition. If a dentist cannot be reached, oral antibiotics (penicillin 500 mg, four times a day) should be started along with warm-water mouth rinses.

DISPLACED TOOTH
If a tooth is knocked out, it may be salvageable if replaced within 30 to 60 minutes.

Treatment
1) Clean the debris off the tooth by rinsing gently (do not scrub!) with saline, milk or disinfected water and gently replace the tooth into the socket. The tooth should be handled only by the crown and not by the root. If the tooth cannot be replaced immediately, it should be stored in a container containing tissue culture medium, saline, milk, or saliva, in that order of preference.

'WEISS ADVICE'
[IMPROVISED TECHNIQUE]

Quick relief of dental pain and bleeding
Bleeding and pain from the mouth can often be relieved by placing a moistened tea bag onto the bleeding site or into the socket that is bleeding.

LOOSE TOOTH
A tooth that becomes loosened, but not displaced, due to trauma should be repositioned with gentle, steady pressure. A soft diet should be maintained to avoid any further trauma until the tooth heals. See a dentist as soon as possible for definitive treatment.

CHEST INJURIES

Because wounds to the chest may interfere with a victim's ability to breathe, he requires immediate medical attention.

BROKEN RIBS

A forceful blow to the chest may break one or more ribs. Broken ribs are very painful and usually require only pain medication and rest.

Signs and Symptoms

1. Pain in the chest which becomes worse when you take a deep breath.
2. A crackling or rattling sensation or sound can occasionally be detected when you touch the broken rib.
3. Rib fractures usually occur along the side of the chest. Pushing on the breastbone (sternum) in the front of the chest while the victim lies on his back will produce pain at the fracture site rather than where you are pushing.

Treatment

Oral pain medication (Motrin® or Vicodin®) will help reduce pain and make breathing easier. It takes about two weeks for pain to subside and four to six weeks for the rib to heal. Taping the chest over the fractured rib may provide added relief from pain.

Chest Injuries

One end of a broken rib can sometimes be displaced inward and puncture the lung producing a pneumothorax (see below). Rib fractures can also bruise the lung or predispose the victim to pneumonia. If a lower rib is fractured, it may injure the spleen or liver and cause severe bleeding. Multiple rib fractures can produce a flail chest (see below). Immediate evacuation to a medical facility is indicated if the victim has more than one rib fracture, develops shortness of breath, difficulty breathing, persistent cough, fever, abdominal pain, or dizziness or lightheadedness upon standing.

FLAIL CHEST

When three or more consecutive ribs on the same side of the chest are broken in two places, a free-floating segment called a "flail chest" can result. The flail segment will move opposite to the rest of the chest during breathing and make it hard for the victim to get enough air. The movement of broken ribs causes great pain, which further reduces the victim's ability to breathe. The underlying lung is usually bruised with a flail chest.

Treatment

1. Immediately evacuate the victim to a medical facility. A flail chest can be tolerated only for the first 24 to 48 hours, before the victim will usually need to be put on a respirator to assist with his breathing.
2. Place a bulky pad of dressings, rolled up extra clothing or a small pillow gently over the site, or have the victim splint his arm against the injury to stabilize the flail segment and relieve some of the pain. Whatever is used should be soft and lightweight. Use large strips of tape to hold the pad in place. Do not tape entirely around the chest as this will restrict breathing efforts. The main function of this object is to make it less painful to breathe, not to stop movement of the chest or restrict

breathing in any manner. If the victim is unable to walk, he should be transported lying on his back or injured side.

3. If the victim is severely short of breath and cannot get enough air, you may need to assist his breathing with mouth-to-mouth rescue breathing. Time your breaths with his, and breathe gently to give him added air with each inspiration.

COLLAPSED LUNG (Pneumothorax)

A collapsed lung (pneumothorax) occurs when air enters the chest cavity and compresses or collapses the lung. This can occur when a broken rib punctures the lung, an outside object such as a knife penetrates the chest, or even spontaneously, when a weak point develops in the lung and permits air to leak into the chest cavity.

Signs and Symptoms
1. Sharp chest pain, which may become worse with breathing;
2. Shortness of breath or difficulty breathing;
3. Reduced or absent breath sounds on the injured side.

Treatment
Evacuate the patient immediately and monitor closely for the development of a tension pneumothorax (see below).

TENSION PNEUMOTHORAX

A pneumothorax can progress to a life-threatening condition called a tension pneumothorax if air continues to leak into the chest cavity. With each breath, air enters the space surrounding the lung, but it cannot escape with expiration. Pressure soon builds up, compressing the lung and heart, which can eventually lead to death.

Signs and Symptoms
1. Labored breathing;
2. Cyanosis (bluish skin discoloration);
3. Signs of shock (weak, rapid pulse, rapid breathing, fear, pale and moist skin, confusion);

4. Distended jugular (neck) veins;
5. Diminished or absent breath sounds on the injured side (place your ear on the chest wall of the victim);
6. Bubbles of air may be felt or heard (Rice Krispies sound) on touching the chest wall or neck.

Treatment

If the situation is desperate and the victim is literally dying before your eyes, there is only one thing that you can do to possibly save his life. You must relieve the pressure from inside the chest (pleural decompression), and allow the lung to re-expand. This procedure takes courage and improvisation in the wilderness. Pleural decompression should not be undertaken lightly and should be attempted only if the victim appears to be dying. The possible complications include infection, profound bleeding from puncture of the heart, lung, or a major blood vessel, or even laceration of the liver or spleen.

HOW TO PERFORM PLEURAL DECOMPRESSION

CAUTION: This technique should only be performed in the wilderness by a trained individual on a victim who would die if the procedure were not done.

1. Swab the entire chest with povidone-iodine or other antiseptic.
2. If sterile gloves are available, they should be put on after the rescuer's hands have been washed.
3. If local anesthesia is available, inject it into the skin at the site to numb the area.
4. Insert a large-bore intravenous catheter (14-gauge), needle, or any pointy, sharp object that is available (the object should not be wider than a pencil) into the chest just above the third rib in the midclavicular line (midway between the top of the shoulder and the nipple, in line with the nipple estimates this location). If you hit the rib, move the needle or pointy object upward slightly until it passes over the top of the rib, thus avoiding the blood vessels that course along the bottom of every rib. A gush of air will signal that you have entered the correct space

and should not push the object in any farther. This will convert the tension pneumothorax into an open pneumothorax.

5. Leave the object in place and put the cut-out finger portion of a rubber glove with a slit cut into the end over the opening to create a one-way flutter valve that allows air out, but not in.
6. Anchor the object to the chest wall with tape so that it cannot be pulled out or forced farther into the chest.
7. If a hole was made with a knife, monitor the victim closely, and if signs of tension redevelop, repeat the procedure above.

OPEN (SUCKING) CHEST WOUND

If an object such as a bullet or knife enters the chest, a wound that opens into the lung can develop. Each time the victim breathes, a sucking sound can often be heard as air passes in and out through the hole.

Signs and Symptoms
1. Painful and difficult breathing;
2. A sucking sound may be heard each time the victim breathes;
3. Bubbles may be seen at the wound site when the victim exhales;
4. Bubbles of air may be felt (crackling sounds) on touching the chest wall near the injury;
5. The patient may develop signs of a tension pneumothorax (see above).

Treatment
1. Seal the opening immediately with any airtight substance and cover it with a 4x4 gauze pad, taping it on three sides. Taping three edges produces a flutter valve effect. When the victim inhales, the free edge will seal against the skin. As he exhales, the free edge will allow air in the chest cavity to escape.
2. If an object is stuck in the chest, do not remove it. Place airtight material next to the skin around it, and stabilize it with bulky dressings or pads. Several layers of dressings, clothing, or handkerchiefs placed on the sides of the object will help stabilize it.

A victim with an open chest wound below the nipple line may also have an injury to an abdominal organ such as the spleen or liver (See next page).

'WEISS ADVICE'

[IMPROVISED TECHNIQUE]

Dressing an open chest wound

An airtight dressing can be improvised from a 4x4 gauze pad impregnated with petroleum jelly, honey, or antibiotic ointment. Saran Wrap or clean plastic will also work. Tape the dressing in place on three sides only.

ABDOMINAL (BELLY) INJURIES

Abdominal organs are either solid or hollow. When solid organs such as the spleen or liver are injured, they bleed internally. Hollow organs can rupture and drain their contents into the abdominal and pelvic cavities, producing a painful and serious inflammatory reaction and infection.

Organ	Type	Location
Liver	Solid	RUQ
Stomach	Hollow	RUQ
Spleen	Solid	LUQ
Pancreas	Solid	LUQ
Small and large intestine	Hollow	All Quadrants
Bladder and Uterus	Hollow	RLQ, LLQ, MLQ
Kidneys	Solid	Flanks

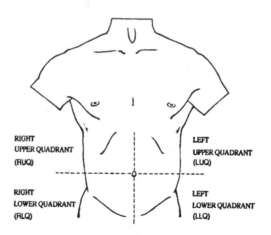

RIGHT
UPPER QUADRANT
(RUQ)

LEFT
UPPER QUADRANT
(LUQ)

RIGHT
LOWER QUADRANT
(RLQ)

LEFT
LOWER QUADRANT
(LLQ)

PENETRATING INJURIES
(See Gunshot Wounds and Arrow Injuries below)

BLUNT ABDOMINAL INJURIES
A blow to the belly can result in internal organ injuries and bleeding, even though nothing penetrates the skin. Examine the abdomen by pressing on it gently with the tips of your fingers sequentially in all four quadrants. Push slowly and observe for pain, muscle spasms or rigidity. Normal abdomens are soft and not painful to touch.

Signs and Symptoms of Internal Abdominal Injures
1. Signs of shock (See page 22);
2. Pain that is at first mild and then becomes severe;
3. Distention (bloating) of the abdomen;
4. Pain, or rigidity (tightness or hardness) of the belly muscles when pressing in on the abdomen;
5. Pain referred to the left or right shoulder tip may indicate a ruptured spleen;
6. Nausea or repetitive vomiting;
7. Bloody urination;
8. Pain in the abdomen on movement;
9. Fever.

Treatment
1. Immediately evacuate the victim to a medical facility.
2. Anticipate and treat for shock.
3. Do not allow the victim to eat. If the victim is not vomiting, he may have small sips of water.

GUNSHOT WOUNDS AND ARROW INJURIES

GUNSHOT WOUNDS

Injuries caused by guns differ in severity and type according to velocity of the bullet, power of the gun, whether fragmentation occurs, presence of powder burns, and type of tissue struck. A gunshot wound may cause severe internal damage and bleeding that is not readily visible or apparent. Although the entrance or exit wound may appear small, the damage inside the body may be great. Any victim who has suffered a gunshot wound should be brought to a medical facility immediately, no matter how minor the external appearance.

General Treatment

1) Follow the basic principles of resuscitation, including airway, breathing, circulation, control of bleeding, immobilization of any broken extremities, wound care, and stabilization of the victim for transport (See page 12).
2) Remove the weapon from the vicinity where you are giving medical care. It may be wise also to remove the ammunition and open the firing chamber.
3) Provide immediate relief of a tension pneumothorax with pleural decompression (See page 40).
4) Treat any sucking chest wound with petrolatum-impregnated gauze (See sucking chest wound, page 42).
5) Control external bleeding with direct pressure and compression wraps.
6) Treat for shock and hypothermia (See page 22).
7) Monitor the neurovascular status of an extremity wound; keep the extremity elevated to minimize swelling.
8) Be aware that the path of the bullet cannot be determined by connecting the entrance and exit wounds.
9) For powder burns, remove as much of the powder residue as possible with a scrub brush because the powder will tattoo the skin if left in place.
10) Expect internal bleeding (see next page).

ARROW INJURY

Arrowheads are designed to inflict injury by cutting tissue and blood vessels, causing bleeding and shock.

General Treatment

1) Follow the same treatment recommendations as for a firearm injury.
2) Stabilize the victim for transport, leaving any embedded arrow in place during transport if possible. Cut the shaft of the arrow and leave about 10 cm (three or four inches) protruding from the wound to make transport easier (see below).
3) Fix the portion of the arrow that remains in the wound with a stack of gauze pads or with cloth and tape.
4) Transfer the victim as quickly as possible to a medical care facility for removal of the arrow under controlled conditions.

DO NOT REMOVE IMBEDDED FOREIGN OBJECTS

If a foreign object (such as a knife, tree limb or arrow) becomes deeply imbedded (impaled) in the body, do not attempt to remove it, because the internal portion may be up against or in a vital organ and acting as a plug, thus preventing further bleeding. Any attempt to remove the object may cause further bleeding and injury. This is particularly true with a hunting (broadhead) arrow. Instead, pad and bandage the wound around the object and secure it in place with tape. The portion of the object that is sticking out of the wound may be cut to a shorter length to facilitate splinting and transport of the victim.

INTERNAL BLEEDING

If bleeding is internal (inside the body), such as from an injured spleen or liver, bleeding ulcer, broken bone, or torn internal blood vessel, the victim may suffer from shock. The symptoms of internal bleeding are the same as those of external bleeding, except that you don't see the blood. They include rapid heartbeat, low blood pressure, shortness of breath, weakness, pale skin color, cool and clammy skin, and confusion. The belly may feel firm to your touch and look distended, and the victim may feel abdominal pain. There may be blood in the vomit, urine or stool. Because it is difficult to predict the rate and severity of internal bleeding, the victim should be brought to medical attention immediately.

SPRAINS

A sprain is the stretching or tearing of ligaments that attach one bone to another. Ligaments are sprained when a joint is twisted or stretched beyond its normal range of motion. Most sprains occur in the ankle and knee. Symptoms include tenderness at the site, swelling, bruising, and pain with movement. Because these symptoms are also present with a fracture, it may be difficult to differentiate between the two.

General Treatment

First aid for sprains is primarily damage control and summarized by the acronym RICES: (Rest, Ice, Compression, Elevation and Stabilization). RICES should be maintained for the first 72 hours after any injury. Too often this is prematurely discontinued after only a few hours.

Rest: Resting takes the stress off the injured joint and prevents further damage.

Ice: Ice reduces swelling and eases pain. For ice or cold therapy to be effective, it must be applied early and for up to 20 minutes at least three to four times a day, followed by compression bandaging. If a compression wrap is not applied after ice therapy, the joint will swell as soon as the ice is removed.

Compression: Compression wraps prevent swelling and provide some support. A compression wrap can be made by placing some padding (socks, gloves, pieces of ensolite pad) over the sprained joint and then wrapping it with an elastic bandage. Begin the wrap toward the end of the extremity and move upward. For example, with an ankle sprain, start from the toes and move up the foot and over the ankle with the wrap. The wrap should be comfortably tight. If the victim experiences numbness, tingling, or increased pain, the compression wrap may be too tight and should be loosened.

Elevation: Elevate the injured joint above the level of the heart as much as possible to reduce swelling.

Stabilization: Tape or splint the injured part to prevent further injury (See below).

Administer a non-steroidal anti-inflammatory medication such as ibuprofen (Motrin®) 400-600 mg three times a day with food to reduce both pain and inflammation.

As soon as possible, seek medical evaluation to determine the need for X-rays to make sure there is no fracture.

ANKLE SPRAIN
Sprained ankles are common backcountry injuries. Most commonly, the ligaments on the outside of the joint are the ones injured when you roll your foot inward (invert) while walking or jumping on an uneven surface.

Treatment
1) First aid begins with RICES.
2) If you cannot bear weight at all, you'll have to splint the foot and ankle **(Fig. 24)** and get assistance out of the backcountry.

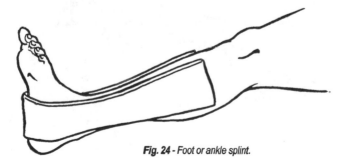

Fig. 24 - Foot or ankle splint.

3) If you can still walk, the ankle should be taped for support with an open basket crossweave stirrup pattern to prevent further injury (**Fig. 25 a & b**).

A) Apply an anchor strip halfway around the lower leg about six inches above the "bumps" in the ankle. Leave a gap of one to two inches between the ends of the tape to allow for swelling.

B) An additional anchor strip can be applied at the instep of the foot. Leave a one to two-inch gap between the tape ends.

C) Apply the first of five stirrup strips. Begin on the inside of the upper anchor, and wrap a piece of tape down the inside of the leg, over the inside bump, across the bottom of the foot, and up the outside part of the leg, over the outside bump, ending at the outer part of the upper anchor.

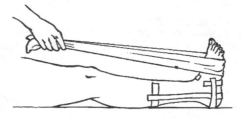

Fig. 25 a & b - Foot or ankle splint.

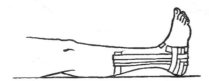

D) Apply the first of six interconnecting horseshoe strips. Start on the anchor on the inside of the foot, and wrap below the inside bump, around the heel, below the outside bump, ending on the anchor on the outer part of the foot.

E) Repeat steps C and D. Remember to overlap the tape one-half its width. These interlocking strips should provide excellent support when walking. After applying these vertical and horizontal strips, there should be a one to two-inch gap on the top of the foot and ankle, which will allow for any swelling.

F) On both sides, secure the tape ends with two vertical strips of tape running from the foot anchor to the calf anchor.

'WEISS ADVICE'

[IMPROVISED TECHNIQUE]

Ankle support with a SAM® Splint

Wrap a Sam® Splint around the foot and ankle, with the shoe in place, and secure it with tape. This will help stabilize the joint while walking. You may need to stop periodically to tighten or rewrap the splint.

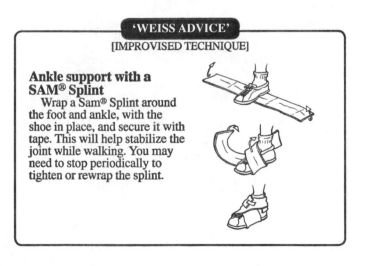

SPRAINED OR RUPTURED ACHILLES TENDON

Running or walking up a hill with a heavy load on your back can injure the Achilles tendon, which attaches your calf muscles to your heel. The tendon can even rupture completely, in which case it pulls away from the bone or snaps in half. If you rupture your Achilles tendon, you'll feel as if someone stabbed the back of your ankle with a sharp object and be unable to bear weight.

Treatment

If the tendon is strained and not completely torn or ruptured, **RICES** is the best treatment. Gently stretch the tendon to keep it flexible, and gradually put weight on the foot, then walk as the pain allows. If you rupture your Achilles tendon, walking will not be possible. The ankle should be splinted and the victim evacuated. Surgery is needed to repair the torn tendon.

KNEE SPRAIN

Twisting, rotating or falling in an awkward position can produce a sprain injury to one of the major ligaments that supports the knee. The collateral ligaments support the sides of the knee, while the anterior and posterior cruciate ligaments support and limit motion in the forward and backward directions. The victim may note an audible crack or a pop at the time of injury, followed by immediate pain that soon turns into a dull ache. The ache may subside after a while, and the knee will swell and feel as though it's going to give way when you put weight on it or turn to the side.

Knee sprains are divided into three degrees of severity based on the amount of ligament that is torn:

First-degree sprains produce pain, but no instability when the knee is stressed, and indicate that only a few ligament fibers are torn. Treatment is initially **RICES** and later physical therapy. Walking can usually be resumed with little or no additional support.

Fig. 26 - *Knee and Leg immobilizer.*

Second-degree sprains produce pain and slight instability when the knee is stressed, and indicate that about half of the ligament fibers are torn. Treatment is the same as for first-degree, but recovery takes longer and surgery may eventually be required. The victim should wear a supportive knee immobilizer while walking **(Fig. 26)**.

Third-degree sprains produce significant instability and indicate a completely torn ligament. Initiate treatment with **RICES** and prohibit walking without a supportive knee immobilizer in place. Even with a third-degree tear, many victims will still be able to walk out of the wilderness with some additional support. If, after applying an improvised knee immobilizer, the knee still feels unstable and prone to buckling with weight, the victim should be evacuated without walking.

'WEISS ADVICE'

[IMPROVISED TECHNIQUE]

Knee immobilizer

A knee immobilizer (knee splint) can be improvised from an ensolite or Thermarest pad, life jacket, newspaper, tent poles or internal pack frame stays and clothing held together with tape or bandannas. The immobilizer should be cylindrical and extend from mid-thigh down to the mid-calf. If possible, cut a circular hole out for the kneecap **(Fig. 26)**.

TORN MENISCI (CARTILAGE)

Menisci are pieces of cartilage that act as shock absorbers for the knee and rest between the thigh and shin bones. Partial and total tears of the meniscus often occur at the same time that ligaments are torn. Pain, localized to one side of the knee joint and made worse by walking, is the most common symptom. Clicking or locking of the knee may be present. Occasionally, the joint can become locked in a partially flexed and painful position, and the victim will not be able to move the knee.

Treatment
  1. Treatment is rest, ice, and ibuprofen (Motrin®) 400 mg
    three times a day with meals.
  2. If the knee feels unstable, wrap a protective immobilizer
    around it (See page 77).
  3. If the victim has a locked knee, attempt to unlock the
    knee by positioning the victim with the leg hanging
    over the edge of a table or flat surface with the knee in
    approximately 90 degrees of flexion. After a period of
    relaxation, the rescuer should apply in-line traction to
    the leg with inward and outward rotation in an attempt to
    unlock the joint. Pain medications and muscle relaxers
    (if available) may facilitate this.

'WEISS ADVICE'

[IMPROVISED TECHNIQUE]

Patella Tendon Band
  To improvise a patella tendon band, roll a bandanna or
triangular bandage tightly in its long axis. Wrap this around
the leg just below the kneecap and tie it securely.

PATELLOFEMORAL SYNDROME
  This common overuse syndrome produces a dull, aching
pain under the kneecap or in the center of the knee. The pain
is aggravated by climbing or descending hills, and by sitting
for long periods with the knees bent. The knee may be swollen and Rice Krispies sounds can often be heard when the
knee is flexed and straightened.

Treatment
  Treatment is rest, ice, and anti-inflammatory medication
such as ibuprofen (Motrin®) 400 mg three times a day with
meals. A patella tendon band placed around the leg, below
the kneecap, may help prevent pain during walking (see
below). Use of two trekking or ski poles while hiking will
help absorb impact on the knees.

STRAINS

A strain is an injury to a muscle or its tendon. The tendon connects the muscle to the bone. Strains often result from overexertion, or lifting and pulling a heavy object without good body mechanics. Strains can sometimes be disabling, especially in the back. Symptoms and treatment are the same as for sprains.

Muscle spasms often accompany a strain injury and can be very painful. Muscle relaxers such as Valium®, Flexeril®, or Soma® may be helpful in relieving spasms, but also produce drowsiness and poor coordination.

As a rule of thumb, the following times are required for initial healing of the musculoskeletal system:

- Muscle: 6-8 weeks
- Bones: 6-12 weeks
- Tendons and ligaments: 12-36 weeks (some ligaments may take 12 months or longer to heal)

BACK PAIN

BACK STRAIN

Back pain ranks among the top 10 most common ailments in backpackers. The lower part of the back, the lumbar spine, holds most of the weight of the body, and therefore is most likely to give you problems. Preventing a back injury is a lot easier than trying to recover from one. While on the trail, there are several things you can do to lessen the chances of injuring your back.

Prevention
1) Stretch before lifting your pack, especially in the morning when your muscles are cold and stiff.
2) When putting on a heavy pack, keep your back straight and in a neutral position. Slide your pack onto one thigh and slip one shoulder into a loosened shoulder strap. Roll the pack onto your back and use your legs, not your back and arms, to lift yourself up.
3) When lifting, always keep objects close to the body.

4) Adjust the pack so as much weight as possible is on the
   hip belt, instead of the shoulder straps.
5) Use a walking stick for added balance and support.

Although back pain may be a symptom of a more serious
condition, it is often due to strained muscles.

Treatment
If possible, rest on your back with a pillow under your
knees or on your side with a pillow between your legs for
one to two days before resuming gentle and graded activity.
Extended bed rest and inactivity can actually weaken the
back and delay recovery. Most people with sudden back pain
will recover completely within two to four weeks.

Other Treatments:
1) Anti-inflammatory medication such as ibuprofen
   (Motrin®) 600 mg three times a day (with meals) for five
   to seven days.
2) Application of cold compresses.
3) Gentle massage.
4) Muscle relaxers to relieve muscle spasms (Valium®,
   Flexeril®, Soma®).

WHEN TO WORRY

Back Pain
   If back pain is severe and not made worse with movement
or change in position, it may be due to some other internal
problem such as an aortic aneurysm or kidney infection. You
should see a physician at once. You should also seek medical
attention immediately if you experience shooting pains, or
tingling down the leg, loss of sensation, interference with
bowel or bladder function, or leg or foot weakness.

KIDNEY STONES

Kidney stones are hard deposits that develop in the urinary tract and produce extreme pain that is often felt in the back. They range in size from a grain of sand to a marble. Kidney stones are three times more common in men than in women and typically develop during middle age. Dehydration and a diet high in protein or calcium are predisposing factors.

Signs and Symptoms

Sudden onset of very severe pain, usually starting in the flank area, or one side of the back and radiating to the abdomen or groin, is typical of kidney stone pain. The victim often rolls from side to side in an effort to find a more comfortable position. With appendicitis or other abdominal infections, the victim usually lies still because movement will increase the pain. Other symptoms may include nausea, vomiting, an urge to urinate, and blood in the urine.

Treatment

1) Drink plenty of fluids — at least four liters a day— which may help to flush out the stone and prevent new stones from forming.
2) Administer pain medication to the victim. An excellent medication for kidney stone pain is ibuprofen (Motrin®, Advil®) or other non-steroidal anti-inflammatory drug.
3) Most kidney stones will eventually pass on their own. Occasionally, kidney stones can lead to infection and damage to the kidney.

Kidney Infections

A kidney infection (Pyelonephritis) will often produce back pain and can be mistaken for a back injury (See Urinary Tract Infections, page 110).

FRACTURES

A fracture is any break or crack in a bone. An open, or compound fracture occurs when the overlying skin at the fracture site has been punctured or cut. This can happen when a sharp bone end protrudes through the skin or from a direct blow which breaks the skin as it fractures the bone. The bone may or may not be visible in the wound. A closed fracture is one in which there is no wound on the skin anywhere near the fracture site. A closed fracture can become an open fracture if it is not handled carefully.

Open fractures are more likely to produce significant blood loss than closed ones. The bone is also contaminated by being exposed to the environment and may become infected. An infected bone is very difficult to treat and may cause long-term problems.

How to Tell If a Bone Is Fractured

It may be difficult to differentiate a fractured bone from a sprained ligament or bruised muscle. When in doubt, splint the extremity and assume it is fractured until you can obtain an X-ray.

Signs of a Possible Fracture:

- Deformity. The limb appears in an unnatural position. Compare the injured with the uninjured limb on the opposite side. Look for differences in length, angle or rotation.
- Pain and tenderness over a specific point (point tenderness).
- Inability to use the extremity. For example, someone who twists an ankle and is unable to bear weight should be suspected of having a broken ankle rather than a sprained ankle.
- Rapid swelling and bruising (black and blue discoloration).
- Crepitus (grating). A grinding sensation can sometimes be felt and heard when touching or moving a fractured limb.
- Inappropriate motion. Motion at a point in a limb where no joint exists indicates a fracture.

Treatment: General Guidelines

1) Inspect the site of injury for any deformity, angulation, or damage to the skin. Instead of removing the victim's clothing, cut away the clothing at the fracture site with blunt-tipped scissors. This will prevent excess movement and better protect the victim from the environment.
2) Stop any bleeding with direct pressure.
3) Check the circulation below the fracture site by feeling for pulses and inspecting the skin for abnormal color changes. Pallor (paleness), bluish discoloration, or a colder hand or foot compared with the noninjured side may indicate a damaged blood vessel. Without circulation, a limb can survive for only about six to eight hours. Check sensation by using a safety pin to determine if the sharp sensation is felt equally on both extremities.
4) Because of the force necessary to break a bone, any person with a fracture should be examined carefully for other injuries.
5) Splint all fractures before the victim is moved, unless his life is in immediate danger. Splinting prevents movement of the broken bones, which avoids additional injury to bones, muscles, nerves, and blood vessels. It also reduces pain, prevents a closed fracture from becoming open, and makes evacuating the victim easier.

TREATMENT OF OPEN FRACTURES

Irrigate the wound with large amounts of sterile saline or disinfected water to remove any obvious dirt and then cover it with a sterile dressing. Do not try to realign the bone or push the bone back under the skin unless it is necessary for splinting and evacuation, or if there are signs of diminished circulation, such as coldness, paleness, or blue discoloration of the extremity.

Realignment of an Open Fracture

1) After thorough irrigation of the wound, pull gently on the limb below the fracture site in a direction which straightens it, while someone else holds counter traction on the limb above the fracture.

2) While continuing to hold traction, immediately apply a
   splint to prevent further motion and damage.
3) Cover the wound with a sterile dressing and bandage.

Splinting

In general, a splint should be long enough to incorporate
the joints above and below the fracture. The splint should
be rigid and well-padded. The splint should immobilize the
fractured part in a position of function. Functional position
means that the leg is almost straight with a slight flexion at
the knee (place a rolled up towel behind the knee), the ankle
and elbow are bent at 90 degrees, the wrist is straight or
slightly extended, and the fingers are flexed in a curve as if
one were attempting to hold a can of soda or a baseball.

* Remove all jewelry, such as watches, bracelets, and rings,
  before applying the splint.
* Use plenty of padding, especially at the bony protrusions
  of the wrist, elbow, ankle, and knees.
* Secure the splint in place with strips of clothing, belts,
  pieces of rope, webbing, pack straps, elastic bandages,
  or duct tape.
* Fashion the splint on the uninjured body part first and
  then transfer it to the injured area to minimize discomfort.
* Elevate the injured body part as much as possible after
  splinting to minimize swelling.
* Always check the circulation after applying a splint or
  doing any manipulation. Check the pulse in the foot or
  wrist, skin color, and temperature often to make certain
  that swelling inside the splint has not cut off circulation.
* Administer any pain medicine that you have to the
  victim.

Realignment of a Closed Fracture
(Fig. 27 a & b)

In general, straightening a fractured limb is not advised,
unless circulation to the extremity is impaired or gross
deformity prevents splinting and transportation. Realignment
is easier if it is done early, before swelling and pain make it
more difficult.

1) Pull gently on the limb below the fracture site in a direction which straightens it, while someone else holds counter-traction on the limb above the fracture. Discontinue the maneuver if the patient complains of a dramatic increase in pain.

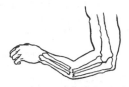

Fig. 27 a & b - Straightening a fracture.

2) After the limb has been straightened, immediately apply a splint before releasing traction. If alignment cannot be achieved, splint the extremity as it lies.

3) After any manipulation, recheck to see whether circulation has been restored or improved.

TREATMENT OF SPECIFIC FRACTURES

NECK AND SPINE

Fractures of the neck and spine can damage the spinal cord and lead to permanent paralysis. Any accident that places excessive force or pressure on the head, neck, or back, such as a fall, head injury, or diving accident, can also result in a fracture of the spine.

The decision to initiate and to maintain spine immobilization in the wilderness has significant ramifications. An otherwise walking victim would require a potentially expensive and arduous rescue. The added delay could worsen other injuries and predispose the victim and the rest of the party to hypothermia or other environmental hazards. Although in general it is always better to err on the side of being overprotective, everyone with a bump or cut on their head does not need to have their spine immobilized.

If a spine injury is suspected, the rescuer should immobilize the head, neck, and trunk to prevent any movement. If the victim is lying in a dangerous location and must be moved quickly, the victim's head and neck should be held firmly by one rescuer's hands, while as many people as available place their arms under the victim from either side. The rescuer at the head says, "Ready, go," and with everyone lifting simultaneously, the victim is lifted as a unit and moved to a safer location. After the victim is moved, one rescuer should continue to hold the head firmly with two hands until the spine is completely immobilized.

If the neck lies at an angle to the body, it should be straightened with gentle in-line traction. A second rescuer should then place a cervical collar around the neck to provide

---

WHEN TO WORRY

Spinal injury

Suspect a spinal injury, and initiate and maintain spine immobilization, after trauma when:
- The victim is unconscious.
- The victim feels pain in the back of the neck, in the middle of the back, or experiences discomfort when those areas are touched.
- There is numbness, tingling or diminished sensation in any part of an arm or leg.
- There is weakness or inability to move the arms, legs, hands, or feet.
- A victim has an altered level of consciousness (see page 23) or is under the influence of drugs or alcohol.
- A victim has another very painful injury that may distract him from noticing the pain in his neck, such as a femur or pelvic fracture, dislocated shoulder, or broken rib.

some stability. Cervical collars alone do not provide adequate immobilization. After a collar is placed around the neck, plastic bags, stuff sacks or socks filled with sand or dirt, or rolled up towels and clothing should be placed on either side of the head and neck and secured to the head with tape or straps to prevent any side-to-side movement. The rest of the body should then be secured to a flat board to prevent any movement.

'WEISS ADVICE'

[IMPROVISED TECHNIQUE]

Improvised cervical collars

A cervical collar can be improvised by using a Sam® splint, sleeping pad, newspaper, backpack hip belt, fanny pack, sleeping pad, life jacket, or clothing.

SAM® Splint cervical collar

SAM® Splint Cervical Collar

Create a bend in the SAM® Splint approximately six inches from the end of the splint. This bend will form the front support which holds the chin. Place the front support underneath the chin and wrap the remainder of the splint around the neck. Create side supports by squeezing the slack in the splint together to form flares under each ear. Finally, squeeze the back of the splint in a similar manner to create a back support and secure the whole thing with tape

Sleeping Pad Collar

Fold the pad long-ways into thirds and center it over the back of the victim's neck. Wrap the pad around the neck, under the chin, and secure it in place with tape

'WEISS ADVICE'
[IMPROVISED TECHNIQUE]

Improvised cervical collars (cont.)

If the pad is not long enough, extensions can be taped or tied on. Blankets, beach towels, or even a rolled plastic tarp can be used in a similar fashion.

Padded Hip Belt
A padded hip belt taken from a large internal or external frame backpack can sometimes be modified, after removal, to function as a cervical collar. If the belt is too long, overlap the ends and secure them with duct tape.

Clothing
Any bulky item of clothing can be used. Wrap a wide ace-type bandage around the entire item first, to compress the material and to make it more rigid and supportive before placing on the neck.

If the victim must be rolled or turned to place insulation or a spine board under him, or if he is vomiting, log-roll him with the head and body held as a unit (**Fig. 28 a-d**). In the event of a suspected spine injury, it is generally better to send for professional rescue assistance rather than attempt to transport the victim yourself.

Fig. 28a *- Log-rolling a victim with multiple rescuers.*

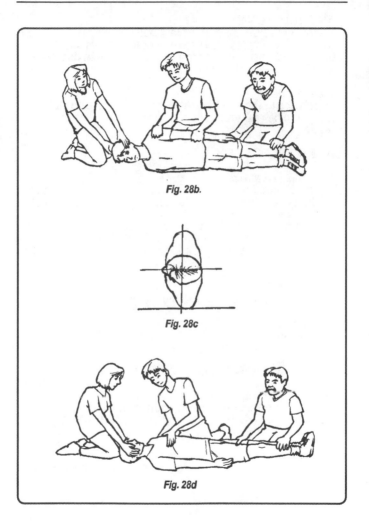

Fig. 28b.

Fig. 28c

Fig. 28d

JAW FRACTURE

A fracture of the mandible (jaw bone) should be suspected if the victim has pain and swelling at the site, is unable to open or close his mouth normally, or if the teeth do not fit together in a normal fashion.

Treatment

Apply ice to the site to reduce swelling and pain. A liquid diet should be maintained until the victim reaches the hospital.

FACIAL FRACTURE

Signs and Symptoms

1) Tenderness to touching the cheek bones or bones around the eyes, swelling and black and blue discoloration of the skin.
2) Grasp the upper teeth between your thumb and forefinger and gently rock the teeth back and forth. Abnormal movement of the upper face when you do this indicates a fracture.
3) The victim may have double vision, especially when he looks upward.
4) The fractured side of the face may feel numb.

Treatment

Elevate the victim's head and apply ice to reduce swelling. Evacuate the victim immediately to a medical facility.

COLLARBONE (CLAVICLE) FRACTURE

This most likely occurs from a fall directly onto the shoulder. The victim will usually hold his arm against the chest wall for support and to prevent motion of the broken bone. The collarbone will be tender to the touch, and there may be a lump or swelling at the site.

Treatment

Splint the arm against the chest with a sling and swath or with safety pins **(Fig. 29)**.

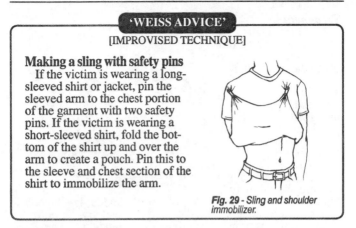

'WEISS ADVICE'

[IMPROVISED TECHNIQUE]

Making a sling with safety pins
If the victim is wearing a long-sleeved shirt or jacket, pin the sleeved arm to the chest portion of the garment with two safety pins. If the victim is wearing a short-sleeved shirt, fold the bottom of the shirt up and over the arm to create a pouch. Pin this to the sleeve and chest section of the shirt to immobilize the arm.

Fig. 29 - Sling and shoulder immobilizer.

Shoulder and Upper Arm (Humerus) Fracture

There is usually pain and tenderness when you touch the site and inability to use the arm. Unlike dislocations of the shoulder, victims with a fracture will still be able to bring the injured arm in tightly and comfortably against the chest and touch their opposite shoulder with the hand of their injured arm.

Treatment

Upper arm fractures should be immobilized with a well-padded splint which extends from the armpit down the inner part of the arm, around the elbow, and back up the outside of the arm to the shoulder. After splinting, secure the arm against the body using a sling and swath or safety pins (Fig. 28). The elbow should be flexed less than 90 degrees to avoid pinching off any blood vessels.

Elbow, Forearm or Wrist Fracture

These usually occur after a fall on an outstretched hand. A broken wrist sometimes has a deformity which makes it look like an upside down fork.

Treatment

1) If there is an obvious deformity and circulation has been cut off to the hand (there is no pulse at the wrist, and the hand is turning blue and cold compared with the uninjured hand), apply firm traction to straighten the deformity.

2) A splint for a wrist, forearm or elbow fracture should include

Fig. 30 - Sam Splint® for elbow, forearm, or wrist fracture.

both the elbow and hand. Apply a well-padded, U-shaped splint, which extends from the hand to the elbow on both sides and wraps around the elbow like a sandwich. The elbow should be bent at 90 degrees, the wrist should be as straight as possible, and the hand should be in a position of function with the fingers curled around something soft such as a rolled up glove, sock, or bandage (**Fig. 30**).

3) After splinting, secure the arm against the body for added support.

'WEISS ADVICE'

[IMPROVISED TECHNIQUE]

The SAM® Splint

The SAM® Splint, a versatile and lightweight padded aluminum splint, is excellent for splinting upper extremity fractures. It goes from being flexible to rigid when bent into a U-shape down its long axis. The SAM® Splint can be used for splinting arms in almost any position. The blue side of the splint, slightly thicker and softer than the orange side, should be placed against the skin.

HAND AND FINGER FRACTURE

Treatment

After removing any jewelry, place a rolled pair of socks or elastic bandage in the palm to keep the fingers curled in a grabbing position (position of function) and secure this in place with an elastic or gauze bandage. Keep the tips of the fingers uncovered in order to check circulation **(Fig. 31)**. Splint a broken finger by buddy-taping the injured finger to an adjacent uninjured finger **(Fig. 32)**. Elevate hand injuries to minimize swelling.

Fig. 31 - Splint for hand fractures.

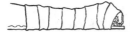

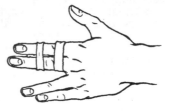

Fig. 32 - Finger splint (Buddy taping fingers)

RIB FRACTURE *(See Chest Injuries)*

PELVIS FRACTURE

Pelvic ring fractures are devastating injuries, often accompanied by extensive internal bleeding that can often be fatal. In addition to losing large amounts of blood into the pelvis from broken bones and torn blood vessels, the victim with a pelvic fracture often has other major internal injuries and bleeding. The victim can go into shock and bleed to death internally without any sign of external bleeding. Organs such as the bladder or intestines may also be damaged.

Signs and Symptoms

There may be pain in the pelvis, hip or lower back and inability to bear weight. Pressing or squeezing gently on the pelvis at the belt line will produce pain. If the broken pelvis is unstable, you may feel the movement of the bones when you compress the pelvis. If you find an unstable pelvis during your assessment, don't do any further exams of the pelvis. Further pressing or squeezing the pelvis can dislodge internal blood clots and cause more bleeding. If the bladder or urethra is damaged, there may be blood at the tip of the penis or in the urine, or the victim may be unable to urinate.

Treatment (Fig 33 a & b)

Stabilization and static compression of the broken pelvis with a pelvic sling or binder will help control bleeding and may save the victim's life. It's a technique that works, even for the worst type of pelvic fractures, known as open-book fractures because the pelvic ring has sprung open like the pages of a book. Compression "closes the book," reduces pain, slows bleeding, and promotes clot formation as the patient is transported to an emergency department.

A commercial product called the SAM Sling™ has been developed by Sam Medical Products, the makers of the SAM Splint™, for pelvic immobilization and stabilization in the field. On long expeditions, or ones far from medical care, it should be included with the medical kit.

Clothes, sheets, sleeping bags, pads, or a tent fly can be used to improvise a pelvic sling in the backcountry. First, remove any objects from the victim's pockets their belts if they are wearing one so that pressure of the sling doesn't cause additional pain by pressing items against the pelvis. Then, slide a sheet, jacket, sleeping pad or other improvised sling under the victim's buttocks and center it under the bony prominences at the outer part of the upper thigh or hips (greater trochanters/symphysis pubis). Cross the object over the front of the pelvis and tighten the sling by pulling both ends and securing with a knot, clamp or duct tape. The sling should be tightened so that it is snug. If an inflatable sleeping pad is used, inflate the pad after securing to increase the pressure exerted on the pelvis.

Place padding between the legs and gently tie the legs together to further stabilize the fracture in a position that is most comfortable for the victim. Treat for shock, but do not elevate the legs. Transport the victim if possible on a well-padded but firm surface, or better yet, arrange for a helicopter evacuation.

 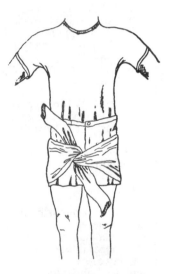

Fig. 33a - A Thermorest or other inflatable mattress or pad can be wrapped around the pelvis as described above and secured with duct tape. Then blow into the valve and infate the pad or mattress as you would for sleeping.

Fig. 33b - Slide a sheet, tent fly, coat or other garment under the victim's buttocks and center it under the bony prominences at the outer part of the upper thigh or hips (greater trochanters/symphysis pubis). Cross the object over the front of the pelvis and tighten the sling by pulling both ends and securing with a knot, clamp or duct tape. The sling should be tightened so that it is snug.

'WEISS ADVICE'
[IMPROVISED TECHNIQUE]

Traction Splint

There are a variety of techniques for improvising a traction splint with limited materials in the backcountry. An improvised traction splint has six components:

1. Ankle hitch;
2. Upper thigh (crotch) hitch;
3. Rigid support that is longer than the leg;
4. Method for securing the two hitches to the rigid support;
5. Method for producing traction (trucker's hitch);
6. Padding.

WARNING: Before applying an improvised splint to the victim, test your creation on a noninjured member of your party or at least the noninjured leg of the victim.

1) Apply an ankle hitch. It is best to leave the shoe on the victim's foot and apply the hitch over it. Cut out the toe of the shoe to periodically check the circulation in the foot.

Double runner stirrup: Fold two long, narrow and strong pieces of material (webbing, triangular bandages or bandannas folded into cravats, pieces of rope, or even shoelaces) into loops and lay one over and one behind the ankle, making sure the ends of each loop are facing in opposite directions (**Fig. 34**). Pull the ends through the loop on both sides. The hitch should fit snugly and flat against the

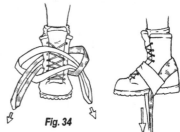

Fig. 34

Double runner stirrup ankle hitch   **Fig. 35**

Traction Splint (cont'd)

ankle. Adjust the two pieces of material so that the ends are centered under the arch of the shoe and the traction is in line with the leg **(Fig. 35)**. The foot should be at a 90-degree angle with the ankle.

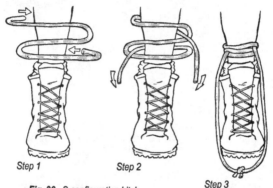

Step 1   Step 2

Step 3

Fig. 36 *- S-configuration hitch*

S-configuration hitch: This type of hitch is preferred if the victim also has an injury to his foot or ankle, because traction is pulled from the victim's calf instead of his ankle. Lay a long piece of webbing or other similar material over the upper part of the ankle (lower calf) in an S-shaped configuration. Wrap both ends of the webbing behind the ankle and up through the loop on the other side. Pull the ends down on either side of the arch of the foot to tighten the hitch and tie an overhand knot **(Fig. 36)**.

Traction Splint (cont'd)

Buck's traction: For
extended transports, this
system is more comfort-
able, but must be checked
periodically for slippage.
Duct tape is wrapped
around a piece of ensolite
or other sleeping pad
to create a stirrup as
shown. The entire unit is
secured to the lower leg
with an elastic or other
improvised bandage. This
system greatly increases
the surface area over

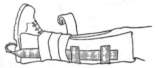

Fig. 37 - Buck's traction.

which traction is applied and decreases the potential
for painful pressure points and compression of blood
vessels leading to the foot **(Fig. 37)**.

2) Apply the Upper Thigh Hitch.
Tightly wrap a rolled up jacket or other material (belt,
webbing, fanny pack, or pack straps) around the upper
part of the thigh and tie an overhand knot. Climbers
can use a climbing harness, while paddlers can use an
inverted life jacket worn like a diaper. Regardless of
the material used, make sure to pad the crotch and inner
thigh.

3 & 4) Apply a Rigid Support to the Outside of the Injured Leg and Secure It Between the Two Hitches
Place a rigid, straight object that is at least a foot
longer than the leg against the outside of the leg and
secure it to the upper thigh hitch with tape or strap-
ping material. You can use one or two ski poles lashed
together with duct tape, a ski, tent poles, canoe or kayak
paddle, or a straight tree branch.

Traction Splint (cont'd)

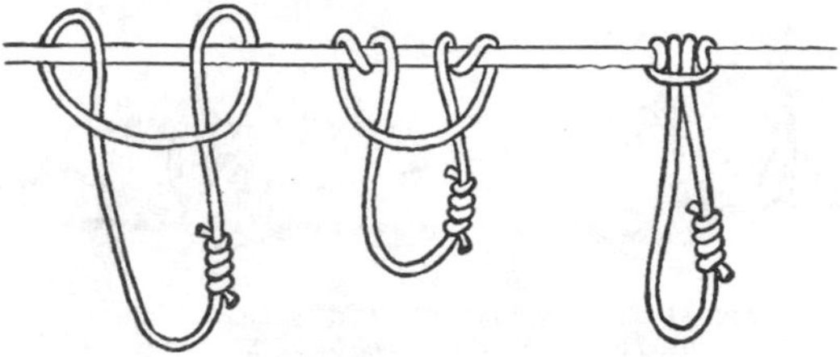

Fig. 38 - Tying a Prusik knot.

Attach the ankle hitch to the rigid support. A blanket pin or bent tent stake can be placed in the end of a tent pole to provide an anchor for the traction system. A Prusik knot (**Fig. 38**) can be used as an attachment point on almost any straight object.

5) *Apply Traction*

The amount of traction required will vary with the individual. A stopping point for pulling traction is when the injured leg looks to be back to its normal length (compare it with the uninjured leg), or when the victim is more comfortable. Use a trucker's hitch to gain mechanical advantage when pulling traction (**Fig. 39**).

After applying traction, check the circulation and sensation in the foot every 30 minutes. If the pulse is lost or diminished with traction, or if the foot turns blue or cold, reduce the amount of traction in the splint until the color and pulse return.

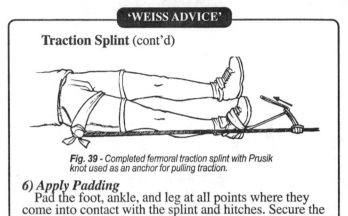

'WEISS ADVICE'

Traction Splint (cont'd)

Fig. 39 - Completed femoral traction splint with Prusik knot used as an anchor for pulling traction.

6) Apply Padding
   Pad the foot, ankle, and leg at all points where they come into contact with the splint and hitches. Secure the entire splint firmly to the leg.

THIGH BONE (FEMUR) FRACTURE

A broken femur can produce severe blood loss and lead to shock. When the femur breaks, the thigh muscles spasm, pulling the thigh into a more spherical shape which allows a greater amount of blood to escape into the surrounding tissues. The broken bone ends will overlap and dig into the muscle, causing additional injury, extreme pain, and further blood loss. Often, the broken leg will appear shortened and the foot may be rotated outward, away from the other leg.

Treatment

The best splint for a femur fracture is one that produces traction to stretch the muscles back to their normal length. This will significantly reduce blood loss, muscle spasms, and pain, and will facilitate evacuation. First, apply traction with your hands by holding the victim's foot and pulling the leg back into normal alignment. Try to pull the injured leg out to its normal length, using the uninjured leg as a guide. Once you have started pulling traction, do not release it. If it's just you and the victim, create a traction splint first, then pull and maintain traction with the device.

KNEE FRACTURES

Fractures around the knee should be splinted from the hip to the ankle with a cylinder splint. You can use a life jacket or rolled up sleeping pad. Individuals with fractures near the knee should not be allowed to walk without crutches.

LOWER LEG (TIBIA AND FIBULA) FRACTURES

Check for deformity, crepitus (grinding sounds), point tenderness and immediate swelling. A victim with a tibia fracture will not be able to bear weight. Some victims with an isolated fibula fracture can still walk painfully on the injured leg.

Treatment

If necessary, apply gentle traction to straighten any deformity that exists in the leg and maintain the traction while another person applies a splint. For lower leg fractures, apply a splint that encompasses the leg from the knee to the ankle. A U-shaped splint running from the inner thigh above the knee around the bottom of the foot and up the outside of the leg back to the knee, with adequate padding, is an excellent splint. After splinting, elevate the leg to reduce swelling. Check the circulation and sensation in the foot every 30 minutes.

'WEISS ADVICE'

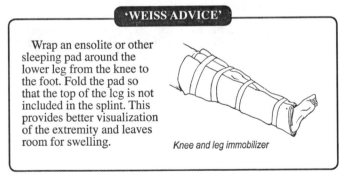

Wrap an ensolite or other sleeping pad around the lower leg from the knee to the foot. Fold the pad so that the top of the leg is not included in the splint. This provides better visualization of the extremity and leaves room for swelling.

Knee and leg immobilizer

ANKLE AND FOOT FRACTURES

It can be hard to differentiate a broken ankle bone from a severe ligament sprain without X-rays. Both can produce swelling, pain, and black-and-blue discoloration. If the victim is unable to bear weight, or if gentle pressure directly on the bony prominences on the inside or outside of the ankle produces severe pain, treat the injury as a fracture.

Treatment

Apply a well-pad-ded splint that begins halfway down the calf and extends around the bottom of the foot and back up the other side, encompassing the ankle like a sandwich. The ankle should be

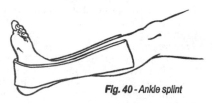

Fig. 40 - Ankle splint

splinted at 90 degrees **(Fig. 40)**. Leave the boot or shoe in place, but remove the tongue so that circulation and sensation can be periodically checked. Keep the foot elevated above the level of the heart as much as possible.

TOE FRACTURES
Treatment

Splint a fractured toe by buddy-taping it to an adjacent toe with small pieces of tape. Place cotton or gauze material between the toes to prevent rubbing and chafing.

DISLOCATIONS

A dislocation is a disruption of a joint in which a bone is pulled out of its socket. Dislocations often damage the supporting structures of the joint and tear ligaments. Sometimes a joint under strain may "pop out" of position and back in again (subluxation). This will be painful, but does not require reduction (relocation or returning to normal position). A subluxation is treated as a sprain injury. Dislocations are most common in the shoulders, elbows, fingers, and kneecap (patella).

The reduction of a dislocation (returning the bone to its normal position) by non-physicians is controversial in wilderness medicine. There are many good reasons for reducing a dislocation in the backcountry, especially when rapid transport to a hospital is not possible:

• Reduction is easier soon after injury, before swelling and muscle spasm develop.
• Reduction relieves pain.
• Early reduction reduces the risk of further injury to blood vessels, nerves, and muscles. Blood vessels can become trapped, stretched or even compressed during a dislocation which leads to loss of blood flow to the limb if reduction is not performed.
• It is easier to splint the extremity and evacuate the victim after reduction.

Even if there is a fracture along with the dislocation, the first step in treatment is to attempt to reduce the dislocation (although a fracture may sometimes prevent you from reducing the dislocation).

If you are unable to reduce the dislocation immediately, administering pain relievers and muscle relaxers, and waiting at least 20 minutes for them to take effect, may make it easier. Use steady, constant traction when attempting a reduction. After any dislocation is reduced, the extremity should be splinted in the same manner as for a fracture. If a dislocation can't be reduced, splint the extremity in the most comfortable position for the victim.

SHOULDER DISLOCATION

Shoulder dislocations are common in kayakers and skiers because paddles and ski poles place added force on the joint. For a shoulder dislocation to occur, the arm is usually pulled away from the body, rotated outwards and extended backwards. This can occur when a kayaker high braces or attempts to roll his boat. The arm gets yanked out of its socket and lodges in front of the joint.

Recognition

Victims are usually in severe pain and aware that something is out of joint. The shoulder may look squared off, lacking the normal rounded contour. The victim will usually hold the arm away from the body with the uninjured arm and be unable to bring it in tightly into his chest. If the victim can bring the arm across the body in a normal position for splinting and touch his opposite shoulder with his hand, then you should assume he does not have a shoulder dislocation.

Treatment

Before attempting to reduce the shoulder, check the pulse in the wrist (radial pulse) and the circulation (temperature, color and capillary refill) in the hand. Check the nerve function by asking the victim to move his wrist up and down and move all of his fingers. Test for sensation to touch or pinprick.

There are many good techniques for reducing a shoulder dislocation. In the backcountry, the key is to do it quickly, before the muscles spasm and while the patient is standing or sitting.

WEISS TECHNIQUE (STANDING)

Have the victim bend over at the waist while you support his chest and allow his arm to hang down toward the ground. Support as much of the victim's weight as possible to allow him to relax. With your other hand grab the victim's wrist and turn the arm slowly so that the palm faces forward. Then apply steady downward traction and very slowly bring the arm forward toward the head (**Fig. 41 a & b**). Avoid jerky movements. You may need to hold traction for a few minutes before it pops back into the shoulder socket.

If two rescuers are available, one should support the victim at the chest and provide counter-traction while the other pulls downward on the arm. The person supporting the chest can also use the thumb of his other hand to push the scapula (shoulder blade) inward toward the backbone (**Fig. 42**). This scapular manipulation maneuver helps position the socket so the arm can slip back in easier. You can usually notice a clunk and shift of the arm as it returns to the joint, combined with a sigh of relief from the victim.

Fig. 41 a & b - One rescuer Weiss Technique (standing) for reducing a dislocated shoulder

Fig. 42 - Two rescuer Weiss Technique (standing) for reducing a dislocated shoulder

WEISS TECHNIQUE (SITTING)

While the victim is sitting, grab his forearm close to his elbow with both of your hands. With the victim's elbow bent at 90 degrees, pull steady downward traction on the arm by pulling on his forearm. After about a minute of sustained traction, slowly raise the entire arm upward, until reduction is complete.

Fig. 43 - One rescuer sitting technique for reducing a dislocated shoulder

Gingerly rotating the forearm outward while pulling traction may facilitate reduction. If another rescuer is available, he should provide counter-traction from behind the victim while performing scapular manipulation as described above. **(Fig. 43)**

After the shoulder is reduced, recheck the victim's circulation, sensation and ability to move his fingers and wrist. Immobilize the arm with a sling and swathe bandage.

WARNING: If a dislocated shoulder cannot be reduced after two attempts, or if the reduction maneuver produces a dramatic increase in pain, the attempt should be aborted and the arm splinted in the most comfortable position for the victim.

This usually requires placing a pillow or rolled blanket under the armpit, between the arm and chest wall.

ELBOW DISLOCATION

Recognition

There will be a deformity of the elbow when compared with the uninjured side, and movement of the elbow will be very limited and painful. Check for a pulse in the wrist and determine if the victim can move his fingers and wrist.

Treatment

Elbow dislocations require a great deal of traction and may be impossible to reduce in the backcountry. If you are unable to reduce the dislocation, splint the arm in the most comfortable position for the victim. To attempt reduction, have the victim lie on his stomach with the elbow bent at 90 degrees over the padded edge of a table or ledge. Pull downward on the wrist while another rescuer pulls upward on the upper arm. Rocking the forearm back and forth gently may help the reduction.

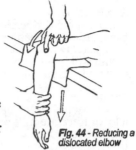
Fig. 44 - Reducing a dislocated elbow

After any reduction attempt, recheck the pulse in the wrist and circulation to the fingers (**Fig. 44**).

After reduction, the elbow should be splinted as though it were a fracture (See page 68).

FINGER DISLOCATION

Recognition

There victim will be unable to move the dislocated joint and there will be an obvious deformity. Do not attempt to reduce a dislocation at the base of the index finger. Splint this injury in a position of comfort and seek medical attention.

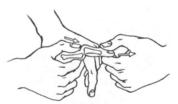
Fig. 45 - Reducing a dislocated finger

Treatment

Pull on the tip of the finger with one hand, while pushing the base of the dislocated finger with the other hand (**Fig. 45**). After reduction, buddy-tape the reduced finger to an adjacent finger (**Fig. 46**).

Fig. 46 - Buddy tape the finger

HIP DISLOCATION

Recognition

In most hip dislocations, the femur is pushed out and back, dislodging behind the pelvic socket. The victim's leg is rotated inward, and the hip and knee are both flexed. The victim will be in a great deal of pain and be unable to move or straighten the injured leg.

Treatment

Two people and a lot of force are required to reduce a pelvic dislocation. Place the victim on his back with the knee and hip both flexed at 90 degrees. One rescuer will hold the victim flat on the ground by pushing down with his hands on both sides of the victim's pelvic bone. The

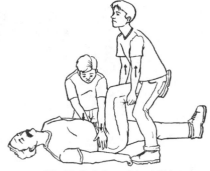

Fig. 47 - Reducing a dislocated hip

other rescuer straddles the victim's calf, locks his hands behind the victim's knee, and applies steady traction in an upward direction **(Fig. 47)**. Reducing a hip is often difficult and requires a great deal of prolonged pulling to overcome the powerful leg muscles.

Once reduced, the injured leg should be splinted to the un-injured leg and the victim transported to a medical facility. If reduction is unsuccessful, splint the leg in the most comfortable position for the victim, and arrange evacuation.

KNEECAP (PATELLA) DISLOCATION

Dislocation of the kneecap usually occurs from a twisting injury while the knee is extended. The kneecap is displaced to the outer part of the knee, resulting in an obvious deformity and pain. The knee is usually flexed and the victim is unable to move it.

Treatment

A patella dislocation can usually be reduced by pushing the kneecap back toward the inside of the knee with your thumbs, while gently straightening the leg **(Fig. 48)**. The kneecap will pop back into place and there should be immediate relief of pain. If the maneuver is very painful or not easily accom-

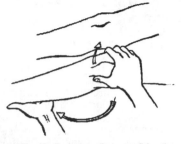

Fig. 48 - Reducing a knee cap dislocation

plished, do not continue with the attempt. After the kneecap is repositioned, the victim should be able to walk with an improvised knee immobilizer. If you're unable to reduce the patella, splint the knee in a position of comfort and evacuate the victim.

KNEE DISLOCATION

Do not confuse this devastating injury with a dislocation of the kneecap. A total knee dislocation results in the disruption of all of the ligaments of the knee and a very unstable joint. Often the knee will reduce itself spontaneously. If the knee is still deformed, gently reposition and straighten it by applying gentle traction to the lower leg. The victim should be evacuated immediately to the nearest medical facility. A major artery in the leg is often torn or damaged during the dislocation, and if not repaired within six to eight hours, the leg may need to be amputated.

ANKLE DISLOCATION

Sometimes a severe ankle fracture can also be dislocated. Apply gentle traction to the foot and ankle until the deformity has been corrected and the ankle is better aligned. Splint the ankle as you would for a fracture (See page 78).

WOUNDS (CUTS AND ABRASIONS)

BLEEDING

Almost all bleeding can be stopped by applying direct pressure to the wound. Use whatever clean material is available to hold pressure on the bleeding site. Then, as time allows, use sterile gauze from your first-aid kit. The idea is not to soak up blood with a big wad of bandage, but to apply firm pressure directly on the bleeding site. If direct pressure does not stop the bleeding, examine the wound to make sure you are holding pressure on the correct spot before putting more bandages on top of those already in place. It might be necessary to hold pressure for up to 30 minutes to prevent further bleeding. If you need to free up your hands, create a pressure dressing by wrapping an elastic bandage tightly around a stack of 4x4 gauze pads placed over the wound.

If bleeding from an extremity cannot be stopped by direct pressure, and the victim is in danger of bleeding to death, apply a tourniquet. A tourniquet is any band applied around an arm or leg so tightly that all blood flow beyond the band is cut off. If the tourniquet is left on for more than three hours, everything beyond the tourniquet will die, and that part of the arm or leg may require amputation (See page 8).

Never apply direct pressure to a bleeding neck wound because it can interfere with breathing. Instead, carefully pinch the wound closed. Never apply direct pressure to the eye, either, because you could cause permanent damage.

'WEISS ADVICE'

[IMPROVISED TECHNIQUE]

Stopping the bleeding

Afrin® or Neo-Synephrine® nasal spray contains potent blood vessel constrictors and may help stop wound bleeding. Simply moisten a 4x4 piece of gauze with the solution, and then pack the gauze into the wound. Henry Herrmann, an authority on wilderness dentistry, recommends using tea bags to control bleeding in the mouth. The tannic acid in tea acts as a vasoconstrictor and can even help relieve pain.

Anytime you deal with blood, it's vitally important to protect yourself from blood-borne pathogens, such as hepatitis and the AIDS virus, by wearing barrier gloves. Even latex gloves can leak, so make sure to wash your hands or wipe them with an antimicrobial towelette after removing the gloves. Dispose of bloody gloves and bandage materials by securing them in a waterproof bag.

CLEANING

The moment skin is broken, bacteria begin to multiply inside the wound, and any blood or damaged tissue left behind will create a feeding ground for hungry germs. The goal of wound cleansing, therefore, is to rid the wound of as much bacteria, dirt and damaged tissue as possible.

The best cleansing method is to use a 10 to 15-ml syringe with an 18 or 19-gauge catheter tip attached to the end to create a high-pressure irrigation stream (see below). Using the syringe like a squirt gun creates an ideal pressure, forceful enough to flush out germs and debris without harming tissues.

Disinfected water is ideal for irrigating wounds. Water can be quickly disinfected by adding 10 ml of Betadine® (10% Povidone-Iodine) solution to one-half liter of backcountry water and allowing it to sit for five minutes. If the water is particularly dirty, pour it through a coffee filter, bandanna or paper towel before disinfecting.

Hydrogen peroxide should not be poured into wounds because it is damaging to tissue and can delay healing. Even full-strength Betadine® (10% Povidone-Iodine) solution is toxic to delicate skin tissues and shouldn't be poured directly into a wound unless diluted first.

HOW TO IRRIGATE A WOUND (Fig. 49 a-c)

Draw the disinfected water into the syringe and attach an 18-gauge catheter tip. Hold the syringe so the catheter tip is just above the wound and perpendicular to the skin surface. Push down forcefully on the plunger while prying open the edges of the wound with your gloved fingers, and squirt the solution into the wound. Be careful to avoid getting splashed by the solution as it hits the skin (put on sunglasses or

Fig. 49 a-c - Wound irrigation

goggles to help protect your eyes from the spray). Repeat this
procedure until you have irrigated the wound with at least
400 ml of solution. The more you use the better.
Remember: "The solution to pollution is dilution."

Inspect the irrigated wound for any residual particles of dirt
or dried blood and, if present, carefully pick them out with
tweezers. This is crucial because even one or two particles of
dirt left in a wound will increase the likelihood of infection.
Any renewed bleeding should again be controlled by direct
pressure.

'WEISS ADVICE'

[IMPROVISED TECHNIQUE]

Wound irrigation with a plastic bag & safety pin

Fill a plastic sandwich or
garbage bag with disinfected
water and puncture the bottom of the bag with a safety
pin or pointy knife. Hold the
bag just above the wound
and squeeze the top firmly to
begin irrigating.

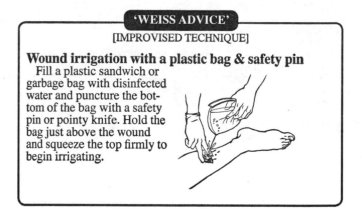

WOUND CLOSURE

Many cuts can be closed safely in the backcountry. Time is a critical factor, however, and the longer you delay closure, the more likely the wound is to become infected after it is closed. The golden period for closing most wounds is within eight hours after the injury occurs. If you wait longer, bacteria multiply inside the wound to a dangerous level and swelling progresses, interfering with the body's defense system. Wounds on your face or scalp can be closed up to 24 hours later, because these areas are more resistant to infection.

Some wounds always carry a high risk of infection, regardless of when they are closed. Examples are wounds inflicted by animal or human bites, puncture wounds, deep wounds on the hands or feet and those that contain a great deal of crushed or damaged tissue.

Most high-risk wounds, and those that have aged beyond the golden period, are best left open and packed with 4x4 gauze dressings moistened with saline solution or disinfected water. Cover the packed wound with a bandage and splint the extremity. Antibiotics, if available, should be taken. The packing should be changed at least once a day, and medical care should be obtained as soon as possible.

Otherwise, the preferred way to close a cut in the backcountry is with the use of wound closure tape strips or butterfly bandages. Wound closure strips are better because they are stronger, longer, stickier and more porous than butterfly bandages.

CLOSING A WOUND WITH WOUND CLOSURE STRIPS

1) Use your scissors to clip off hair near the wound so the tape will adhere better. Hair farther from the wound edge can be shaved. Avoid shaving hair right next to the wound edge as it abrades the skin and increases the potential for infection.
2) Apply a thin layer of tincture of benzoin evenly along both sides of the wound, being careful to avoid getting the solution into the wound (it stings). Benzoin's stickiness will help keep the tape in place (**Fig. 50**).

3) After the benzoin dries (about 30 seconds), remove a strip of tape from its backing (**Fig. 51**) and place the tape on one side of the wound. Use the other end of the tape as a handle to pull the wound closed (**Fig. 52**). Try not to squeeze the wound edges tightly together; they should just touch. Attach the other end of the tape to the skin to keep the wound closed.

Fig. 50

4) The tape should overlap the wound edge by about an inch on each side. More tape can be applied as needed, with a gap of about a half inch between each strip (**Fig. 53**).

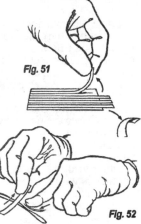

Fig. 51

5) Place pieces of tape crossways (perpendicular to the other strips) over the ends of the existing strips to keep the ends of the tape from curling up (**Fig. 54**).

6) Leave the tape in place 7 to 10 days.

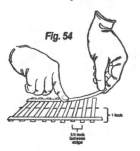

Fig. 54

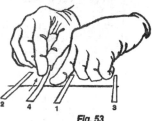

Fig. 52

Fig. 53

1 inch

1/4 inch between strips

'WEISS ADVICE'

[IMPROVISED TECHNIQUE]

Wound closure strips

Wound closure strips can be improvised from duct tape or other adhesive tape. Cut quarter-inch strips, and then puncture tiny holes along the length of the tape with a safety pin to prevent fluid from building up under the tape. If you're without tape, you can even glue strips of cloth or nylon from your clothes, pack or tent to the skin with super glue. Place a drop of glue on the material and hold it on the skin until it dries. Use the other end to the pull the wound closed and glue it onto the skin on the other side of the wound. Avoid getting any glue into the wound. The glue is generally safe on intact skin, but should not be used on the face. Expect the strip to fall off after about two to three days. If you are still in the backcountry, you can reapply more strips with fresh glue.

GLUING A WOUND CLOSED WITH DERMABOND®

Dermabond® (2-octyl cyanoacrylate) is approved by the U.S. Food and Drug Administration (FDA) as a topical skin adhesive to repair skin lacerations. It is packaged as a small single-use applicator. Dermabond® is ideal for backcountry use because it precludes the need for topical anesthesia, is easy to use, doesn't require any needles, and takes up a lot less room in a backpack than a conventional suture kit. Ask your physician to supply you with one for your wilderness outings. Over-the-counter tissue glues (Liquid Bandage™, Nexcare™ Liquid Bandage Drops) can also be used, but they are not as strong an adhesive as Dermabond®, and the wound edges are less likely to stay shut. When applied to the skin surface, Dermabond® will keep wound edges stuck together for three to four days, and peels off without leaving evidence of its presence. Do not substitute Krazy Glue® or SuperGlue® for Dermabond. These preparations may cause injury to the skin.

GLUING A WOUND CLOSED WITH DERMABOND®
(Fig. 55 a-d)

1. Irrigate to wound with copious amounts of disinfected water.

2. Control any bleeding with direct pressure (the glue will not hold well when it is applied to a bleeding wound).

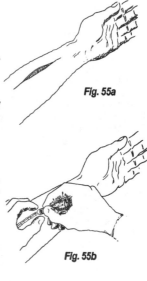

Fig. 55a

3. Tissue glue is applied only to the outside surface of the wound to bridge over the edges; do not apply it directly into an open wound.

4. Gently squeeze the two wound edges together with your fingers so that they are straight, just touching each other, and lie together evenly. Be sure that the wound edges are matched correctly. Hold gauze against downstream areas to catch any drippings as you apply the glue.

Fig. 55b

5. While you hold the edges together, have an assistant paint the tissue glue over the apposed wound edges using a very light brushing motion of the applicator tip. Avoid excessive pressure of the applicator on the tissue because this could separate the skin edges and allow glue into the wound.

6. Apply multiple thin layers (at least three), allowing the glue to dry between each application (about two minutes).

Fig. 55c - *Apply glue between wound closure strips*

7. If the wound is large and

difficult to approximate with your fingers, you can first use wound closure strips (see above) to close the wound edges, and then glue between the strips. Then remove one strip at a time and glue the skin where the strip used to be.

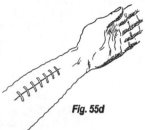

Fig. 55d

8. Glue can be removed from unwanted surfaces with acetone, or loosened from skin with petrolatum jelly.

9. Petroleum-based ointments and salves, including antibiotic ointments, should not be used on the wound after gluing, since these substances can weaken the glue and cause the wound to reopen.

10. After the wound has been glued shut, apply or reapply wound closure strips to back-up your closure (see Closing a Wound With Wound Closure Strips).

Large, gaping cuts and wounds that are under tension or that cross a joint are difficult to tape or glue closed and may require suturing. In these instances, get professional medical care as soon as possible.

SCALP LACERATIONS

Scalp lacerations can often be closed by tying the victim's hair together (See page 26).

DRESS THE WOUND

The best initial dressing is one that won't stick to the wound. Many nonadherent dressings are available over the counter, including Aquaphor®, Xeroform®, Adaptic®, and Telfa®. Allowing the wound to dry out and form a scab will delay healing. A slightly moist environment is preferable to a dry one. Apply a nonadherent dressing

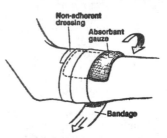

Fig. 56 - Dressing the wound

to the wound, and place an absorbent gauze dressing over the nonadherent one. Hold these both in place with a conforming roller bandage (**Fig. 56**).

CHECK THE WOUND DAILY FOR SIGNS OF INFECTION

Even wounds closed under ideal circumstances have about a five percent chance of becoming infected, so check daily for the following signs of infection:

1) Increasing pain, redness, or swelling;
2) Pus or greenish drainage from the wound;
3) Red streaks on the skin adjacent to or "upstream" from the wound;
4) Fever.

If signs of infection develop, remove the tape and open the wound to allow drainage. Pack the wound with moist gauze daily and consult a physician as soon as possible because antibiotics are usually needed.

ABRASIONS (ROAD RASH)

An abrasion occurs when the outer layer of skin is scraped off. Abrasions are often embedded with dirt, gravel and other debris which, if not removed, can result in scarring or infection.

An abrasion must be vigorously scrubbed with a surgical brush or cleansing pad until all foreign materials are removed. This can sometimes be more painful than the accident itself. It helps to first spread a topical anesthetic,

'WEISS ADVICE'

[IMPROVISED TECHNIQUE]

Making a non-adherent dressing

A nonadherent dressing can be made by spreading polysporin or another antibiotic ointment over one side of a 4x4 gauze dressing. Honey can also be used in place of polysporin. When applied topically, it can reduce infection and promote wound healing.

A conforming roller bandage can be improvised from a shirt or other article of clothing by cutting a thin strip of material in a circular fashion.

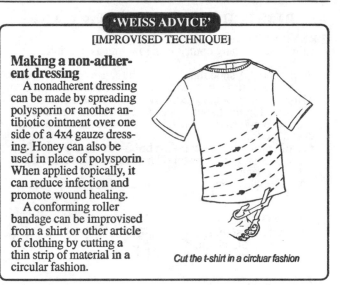

Cut the t-shirt in a circluar fashion

such as 4% Xylocaine® jelly, over the wound or wipe the area with a cleansing pad containing lidocaine. Use tweezers to pick out any remaining embedded particles and then irrigate the abrasion with saline solution or water. A thin layer of aloe vera gel applied to the abrasion after cleaning will reduce inflammation and promote healing.

After cleansing, apply a nonadherent, protective dressing and secure it in place with a bandage. Spenco 2nd Skin® works well because it soothes and cools the wound while providing an ideal healing environment. You can secure it with a stockinette or nonwoven adhesive knit bandage and leave it in place for several days, as long as there is no sign of infection.

BLISTER PREVENTION & CARE

PREVENTION
Eliminate as many contributing factors as possible:
• Make sure that
  fit properly. A shoe that is too tight causes pressure sores;
  one that is too loose leads to friction blisters.
• Break in new boots gradually before your trip.
• Wear a thin liner sock under a heavier one. Friction will
  occur between the socks, instead of between the boot
  and the foot.
• Avoid prolonged wetness. It breaks down the skin,
  predisposing it to blisters. Dry feet regularly and use
  foot powder.
• Apply moleskin to sensitive areas where blisters commonly occur before hiking.

HOT SPOTS
Hot spots are sore, red
areas of irritation which, if
allowed to progress, develop
into blisters.

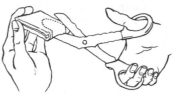

    1) Take a rectangular
piece of moleskin (soft
cotton flannel with
adhesive on the back)
or molefoam, which is
thicker and somewhat
more protective than
moleskin, and cut an oval-
shaped hole in the middle
(like a doughnut) the size
of the hot spot **(Fig. 57)**.

Fig. 57 - Preparing molefoam

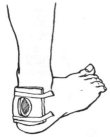

    2) Center this over the hot
spot and secure it in place,
making sure that the sticky
surface is not on irritated
skin. This will act as a buf-
fer against further rubbing
(Fig. 58).

Fig. 58 - Covering a hot spot

3) Reinforce the moleskin with tape or a piece of nonwoven adhesive knit dressing.

'WEISS ADVICE'

[IMPROVISED TECHNIQUE]

Moleskin substitute

If moleskin or molefoam is not available, place a piece of tape over the hot spot (duct tape works well). Molefoam can be even be improvised from a piece of padding from a backpack shoulder strap or hip belt, while a piece of material from the cuff of a sweatshirt or flannel shirt can be used as moleskin.

Treatment of Small, Intact Blisters
1) If the blister is small and still intact, do not puncture or drain it.
2) Place a piece of moleskin or molefoam with a doughnut style hole cut out slightly larger than the blister over the site. It should be thick enough to keep the shoe from rubbing against the blister. This may require several layers. Secure this with tape.

Treatment of Large or Ruptured Blisters
1) If the bubble is intact, puncture it with a clean needle or safety pin at its base, and massage out the fluid. The fluid contains inflammatory juices that can delay healing.
2) Trim away any loose skin from the bubble with scissors.
3) Clean the area with an antiseptic towelette or soap and water.
4) Apply antibiotic ointment or aloe vera gel, and cover with a nonadherent dressing or a gauze pad. Spenco 2nd Skin®, PolyMedica's Spyroflex®, Compeed hydrocolloid dressing® and Elasto-Gel® from Southwest Technologies are all excellent, but more expensive blister dressings.
5) Place a piece of molefoam, with a hole cut out slightly larger than the blister, around the site. Secure everything with tape or a piece of nonwoven adhesive knit dressing. Change the dressing daily or every other day. First applying benzoin to the skin around the blister will help hold the molefoam in place.

6) Inspect the wound daily for any sign of infection. This includes redness around the wound, swelling, increased pain, or cloudy fluid collecting under the dressing. If this occurs, remove the dressing to allow drainage. Consult a physician as soon as possible.

'WEISS ADVICE'
[IMPROVISED TECHNIQUE]

Gluing a blister back in place

If you are far from help, must continue walking, and only have a tube of super glue or benzoin, consider this option: Drain the fluid from the blister with a pin or knife and inject a small amount of glue or benzoin into the space that you have evacuated. Press the loose skin overlying the blister back in place and cover the site with tape or a suitable dressing. The extreme pain this produces will only last a few minutes.

BURNS

The severity of the injury is related to the size and depth of the burn, and the part of the body that is burned. First-aid treatment and the necessity for evacuation are based on the overall burn size in proportion to the victim's total body surface area (TBSA).

The size of the burn injury can be estimated by the Rule of Nines or the Rule of Palms.

RULE OF NINES (ADULTS)
1. Each upper extremity = 9% of TBSA.
2. Each lower extremity = 18% of TBSA.
3. Front and back of trunk each = 18% of TBSA.
4. Head and neck = 9% TBSA.
5. Groin = 1%.

RULE OF PALMS:
An individual's palm covers an area roughly equivalent to one percent of his or her body surface area. Use the size of the victim's palm as a measure to estimate the percentage of body area burned.

General Treatment
1. Apply cool water to the area. Do not over-cool the victim and produce hypothermia. Ice should not be used except on very small burns.
2. Assess the airway and do primary and secondary surveys.
3. Remove all burned clothing from the victim.
4. Remove any jewelry from burned hands or feet.
5. For chemical burns, flush the site with large amounts of water for at least 15 minutes.
6. A victim with a burn greater than 20 percent TBSA can lose a great deal of fluids from burned tissues and go into shock. If he is not vomiting and has a normal level of consciousness, encourage him to drink fluids.
7. Burns less than five percent TBSA (excluding second-degree burns of the face, hands, feet, genitals, or those that completely encircle an extremity) can be treated in the wilderness if adequate first-aid supplies are available and wound care is performed diligently.

FIRST-DEGREE BURNS (SUPERFICIAL BURNS)

Recognition
Only the outermost layer of skin is involved. There is redness of the skin and pain, but no blisters are present. Sunburn is an example, as are most spilled-coffee burns.

Treatment
1 Cool the burn with wet compresses (do not use ice directly).
2. Apply aloe vera gel topically to the burn.
3. Anti-inflammatory drugs (ibuprofen 600 mg three times a day with meals for three days) will provide pain relief and speed healing.
4. First-degree burns rarely require evacuation.

'WEISS ADVICE'

[IMPROVISED TECHNIQUE]

Covering Burns
A gauze pad impregnated with honey is an effective covering for burns. It reduces infection and promotes healing of the wound.

SECOND-DEGREE BURNS (PARTIAL THICKNESS BURNS)
This is a deeper burn, resulting in both redness and blistering. Blisters may not occur for several hours following injury. The burned area is quite painful and sensitive to touch.

Treatment
1. Irrigate the burn gently with cool water to remove all loose dirt and skin.
2. Peel off or trim any loose skin with scissors.
3. Large (greater than 2.5 cm), thin, fluid-filled blisters should be drained and the dead skin trimmed away. Small, thick blisters may be left intact.

4. Apply aloe vera gel or antibacterial ointment to the burn.
5. Cover the burn with a nonadherent dressing such as Spenco 2nd Skin®, Telfa, or Xeroform. Change the dressing at least once a day.

THIRD-DEGREE BURNS (FULL THICKNESS)

Third-degree burns involve all layers of the skin, including nerves, blood vessels, and even muscle. Although these are the most serious burns, they are not painful because the nerve endings have been destroyed. The skin next to a third-degree burn may have suffered only a second-degree burn and still be painful. The appearance is usually dry, leathery, firm, and charred when compared with normal skin, and insensitive to light touch or pinprick. Third-degree burns require skin grafting.

Treatment
1. Same as for second-degree burns.
2. Watch for shock.
3. Immediately evacuate the victim to a burn center.

WHEN TO WORRY

Severe Burns

Severe burns that can lead to shock and require emergent evacuation to a medical center include second-degree burns greater than 20 percent TBSA; third-degree burns greater than 10 percent TBSA; burns involving the hands, face, feet, or genitals; burns complicated by smoke inhalation; electrical burns; or burns in infants and the elderly.

People with facial burns, singed nasal hairs, carbonaceous sputum, hoarseness, or wheezing should be evacuated immediately. They are in danger of developing an obstructed airway from severe swelling in their throat and windpipe.

MEDICAL EMERGENCIES
RESPIRATORY INFECTIONS

TONSILLITIS ("STREP THROAT")

Signs and symptoms that suggest a bacteria (rather than a virus) is the cause of a sore throat include high fevers (over 102 degrees), exudate or pus in the back of the throat, muffled voice, and enlarged lymph nodes in the neck. Bacterial sore throats are treated with antibiotics, such as penicillin or erythromycin.

WHEN TO WORRY

Tonsillitis
   If the victim cannot swallow his saliva or open his mouth fully, he should be evacuated immediately to a medical facility for treatment. Antibiotics, if available, should be administered en route (See appendix).

SINUS INFECTION (SINUSITIS)

Infection of the sinuses may accompany a cold or hay fever. The most prominent symptom is a frontal headache or feeling of heaviness above the eyes or adjacent to the nose. Drainage into the nose or back of the throat, nasal congestion, low-grade fever and tenderness with pressing over the infected sinus are clues to a sinus infection. Pain may be felt in the upper jaw or teeth.

Treatment

Antibiotics (amoxicillin, Zithromax®, Septra®, doxycycline), decongestants, and antihistamines are recommended. The victim should seek medical care as soon as possible.

MIDDLE EAR INFECTION (OTITIS MEDIA)

Symptoms include throbbing or stabbing pain in the ear, decreased or muffled hearing, and fever. Occasionally, a yellow discharge may drain from the ear.

Treatment
Treatment consists of an oral antibiotic (amoxicillin or Septra DS®) for 10 days, and a decongestant such as Sudafed®.

"SWIMMER'S EAR" (OTITIS EXTERNA)
Swimmer's ear is an infection of the outer ear caused by water and bacteria. The first sign is usually itching and vague discomfort in the ear canal. Within a few hours to a day, the ear can become red and extremely painful and drain yellowish fluid. Victims will have increased pain when you pull on the ear lobe or push against their outer ear.

Treatment
Antibiotic ear drops containing polymyxin B and neomycin, or colistin sulfate with hydrocortisone (Cortisporin Otic Suspension®), should be placed into the outer ear canal four times for four to five days. Keep all water out of the ear for two to three weeks.

BRONCHITIS
Bronchitis is an infection of the air passages leading from the windpipe to the lungs. It is often caused by the same viruses that are responsible for colds. The major symptom is a cough that may be dry or productive of yellow or greenish phlegm. Pain in the upper chest, which worsens with coughing or deep breathing, is sometimes present. Victims with bronchitis usually are not short of breath and do not have a rapid respiratory rate.

Treatment
1) Cough expectorants that help bring up phlegm may be helpful. Cough suppressants such as codeine, which impair the body's normal process for expelling phlegm, should be reserved for nighttime use to allow for better sleep.
2) Drink plenty of fluids to help thin the mucus and make it easier to expel.
3) Most cases of bronchitis are caused by viruses, which do not respond to treatment with antibiotics.

WHEN TO WORRY

Bronchitis
If you develop shortness of breath, fever above 101 degrees, wheezing, severe pain in the chest, or a cough producing blood-specked or greenish phlegm, you should see a physician as soon as possible.

PNEUMONIA

Pneumonia is an infection of the lungs produced by either a bacteria or virus, or by physical or chemical agents. Symptoms include a cough that usually produces green or yellowish phlegm, fever, shaking chills, and weakness. Stabbing chest pain, often made worse with each breath, shortness of breath, and rapid breathing may also occur.

Treatment

Antibiotics (amoxicillin, erythromycin, Zithromax®, Septra®, Keflex®, Cipro® or Levaquin®) and professional medical care are needed.

SEIZURES

Seizures (or convulsions) can result from drugs, head injury, heat illness, low blood sugar, epilepsy, fever in children, or other causes. Normally, a grand mal (full body) seizure lasts two to three minutes, during which the victim is unresponsive. When the seizure ends the victim will be sleepy and confused, and should be assisted to professional medical attention as soon as possible.

Treatment

1) Do not try to restrain convulsive movements.
2) Move harmful objects out of the way.
3) Make sure the airway is clear and the victim is breathing. If he is not breathing, start mouth-to-mouth rescue breathing.
4) Roll the victim onto his side to protect the airway if vomiting occurs.
5) Do not put anything in the victim's mouth.

INSULIN SHOCK AND DIABETIC KETOACIDOSIS

If a diabetic becomes confused, weak, or unconscious for no apparent reason, he may be suffering from insulin shock (low blood sugar) or diabetic Ketoacidosis (high blood sugar).

INSULIN SHOCK (LOW BLOOD SUGAR)

If a diabetic takes too much insulin or fails to eat enough food to match his insulin level or his level of exercise, a rapid drop in blood sugar can occur. Symptoms may come on very rapidly and include an altered level of consciousness, ranging from slurred speech, bizarre behavior, and loss of coordination, to seizures and unconsciousness.

Treatment

If still conscious, the victim should be given something containing sugar to drink or eat as rapidly as possible. This can be fruit juice, candy, or a nondiet soft drink. If the victim is unconscious, place sugar granules, cake icing, or Glutose® paste from your first aid kit under his tongue, where it will be rapidly absorbed.

DIABETIC KETOACIDOSIS (HIGH BLOOD SUGAR)

Diabetic ketoacidosis (formerly called diabetic coma) comes on gradually and is the result of insufficient insulin. This eventually leads to a very high sugar level in the victim's blood. Early symptoms include frequent urination and thirst. Later, the victim will become dehydrated, confused, or comatose, and will develop nausea, vomiting, abdominal pain, and a rapid breathing rate with a fruity odor to his breath.

Treatment

The victim needs immediate evacuation to a medical facility. If vomiting is not present and the victim is awake and alert, have him drink small, frequent sips of water. If you are unsure whether the victim is suffering from insulin shock (low blood sugar) or ketoacidosis (high blood sugar), it is always safer to assume it is low blood sugar and administer sugar.

HEART ATTACK

A heart attack occurs when the blood supply to the heart muscle is reduced or completely blocked due to an obstruction in one of the arteries that supply blood to the heart. If blood flow is not restored within one to six hours, part of the heart muscle will die.

Signs and Symptoms
The primary symptom of a heart attack is chest pain. The pain is usually a pressure, crushing, tightness, or squeezing sensation located in the center of the chest, and may radiate up into the neck and jaw or shoulders or down the arms. Sometimes the victim experiences a burning sensation in his lower chest near the solar plexus or a feeling of indigestion. Cold sweats, nausea, vomiting, anxiety, shortness of breath, and weakness are often present.

Treatment
1) Administer one aspirin tablet (325 mg) to the victim. Have him either chew or swallow the tablet. Aspirin may help to partially open the blocked artery.
2) If the victim has nitroglycerin tablets, let him take them as prescribed.
3) If available, administer oxygen and pain medication to the victim.
4) Keep the victim in a comfortable position.
5) Arrange immediate evacuation to a medical facility with the patient doing as little of the work as possible.

STROKE

A stroke is a life-threatening event in which an artery to the brain bursts or becomes clogged by a blood clot, cutting off the supply of oxygen to a part of the brain. A stroke can affect the senses, speech, behavior, thought patterns, and memory. It may also result in paralysis, coma, and death.

Signs and Symptoms
Any or all of the following may occur:
- Sudden weakness or numbness of the face, arm, and leg, usually on one side of the body. One side of the victim's mouth may appear to droop.

- Loss of speech or trouble talking or understanding speech.
- Loss of vision in only one eye.
- Sudden dizziness or loss of coordination.
- Sudden onset of a severe headache.

Treatment
The victim should be transported immediately to a medical facility. Continually reassess the victim's airway and level of consciousness, as his condition can dramatically worsen during transport.

ABDOMINAL PAIN ("BELLYACHES")

Abdominal pain can be due to many causes, including constipation, gas, infection, inflammation, internal bleeding, ulcers, and obstruction or aneurysms of major blood vessels. Abdominal pain can sometimes also be caused by pneumonia, a heart attack, kidney stones (see back pain), or pelvic problems.

WHEN TO WORRY

Abdominal Pain That Requires Urgent Medical Evaluation
Seek medical help for any abdominal pain that lasts longer than four to six hours or is accompanied by frequent or projectile vomiting (vomit that seems to come out under pressure), or fever. Some common causes of abdominal pain that require urgent medical evaluation are appendicitis, ulcer, bowel obstruction, urinary tract and pelvic infections, and any pain during pregnancy.

APPENDICITIS
The appendix is located in the lower right side of the abdomen. Appendicitis occurs when the appendix becomes inflamed and swollen and fills with pus. Appendicitis can occur in persons of any age, but it is most common in young adults.

Signs and Symptoms

The victim usually has a vague feeling of discomfort that often begins in the center of the upper abdomen and within a matter of hours moves to the lower right side. Pain is persistent and steady, but may be worsened by movement, sneezing or coughing. There is usually loss of appetite, nausea, fever, and occasionally vomiting. Pressing on the stomach in the right lower quadrant increases the pain.

Treatment

Transport the victim to a hospital as soon as possible. Do not give the victim anything to eat. If evacuation will take longer than 24 hours and the victim is not vomiting, administer small sips of water at regular intervals (every 15 minutes). If available, administer a broad spectrum antibiotic.

ULCER

An ulcer is an erosion or crater which develops in the lining of the stomach or small intestine.

Signs and Symptoms

An ulcer usually produces persistent burning pain in the center of the upper abdomen, just below the solar plexus. The pain is occasionally relieved by eating and is often associated with nausea and belching. Dark black stools may indicate that the ulcer is bleeding. Sometimes an ulcer can be painless.

Treatment

1) Administer acid-reducing or acid-buffering medication such as Maalox®, Mylanta®, Tagamet® Pepsid® or Zantac®.
2) Avoid taking aspirin or anti-inflammatory drugs such as ibuprofen (Motrin®).
3) Avoid alcohol, spicy foods, and tobacco.
4) Medical evaluation should be obtained as soon as possible.

BOWEL OBSTRUCTION

Bowel obstruction is a blockage of the intestines and occurs most commonly in individuals who have had previous abdominal surgery. It can also develop from infection or other causes.

'WEISS ADVICE'

[IMPROVISED TECHNIQUE]

Ulcer Pain or Heartburn

If you have ulcer pain or heartburn (acid indigestion), and are without any antacids, a glass of cold water alone will sometimes provide relief. A teaspoon or two of mentholated toothpaste, washed down, may provide some relief. Avoid brands with baking soda or hydrogen peroxide.

Signs and Symptoms

Symptoms include nausea, vomiting, and cramping abdominal pain. The victim may have a fecal odor to his breath, and his abdomen may look and feel distended.

Treatment

Evacuate the victim to a hospital. Do not give the victim anything to eat or drink.

GALLSTONES (GALLBLADDER DISEASE)

The gallbladder is connected to the underside of the liver in the upper right part of the abdomen, just below the ribs. Stones can form in the gallbladder and produce an obstruction.

Signs and Symptoms

Pain and tenderness are present in the upper right side of the abdomen. Pushing under the rib cage on the right side of the abdomen while the victim takes a deep breath will increase the pain. The pain may radiate to the shoulder or back. Nausea and vomiting usually occur.

Treatment

Although the condition is not immediately life-threatening, it is best to evacuate the victim to a medical facility as soon as possible. Administer pain medication to the victim and broad-spectrum antibiotics if available. Do not give the victim anything to eat. If evacuation will take longer than 24 hours and the victim is not vomiting, administer small sips of water at regular intervals (every 15 minutes).

URINARY TRACT INFECTIONS

BLADDER INFECTION

If you have to pull off the trail frequently to urinate, and it's painful, then you most likely have a bladder infection. While a bladder infection is not usually a serious disease, it is very uncomfortable and, if untreated, it can spread to the kidneys and produce a potentially dangerous kidney infection.

Women are much more likely to develop a urinary tract infection than men, because the tube that drains the bladder in women (urethra) is much shorter. The short female urethra allows infection-causing bacteria a shorter, easier trip to the bladder, where they can multiply and produce an infection.

Prevention

1) Drink plenty of fluids, to maintain a clear-looking urine.
2) After going to the bathroom, women should wipe themselves from front to back to avoid contaminating the urethral entrance with bacteria from the bowels.
3) Don't postpone urinating when you feel the urge to go.
4) Urinate immediately after sexual intercourse. This helps flush out any bacteria that may have accidentally been pushed into the urethra.
5) In hot or humid conditions, wear loose-fitting pants and wipe the perineal area frequently with moist towelettes.
6) Drinking cranberry juice may help prevent bladder infections. Cranberry juice appears to inhibit the adherence of certain bacteria to bladder cells. Unfortunately, other fruit juices have not been found to share this medicinal quality.

Signs and Symptoms

- Burning pain upon urination;
- Urgent need to urinate frequently;
- Cloudy, bloody, or bad smelling urine;
- Dull pain in lower abdomen.

Treatment
Most bladder infections can be treated with a three-day course of antibiotics such as Septra®, Bactrim® or Cipro®. Another prescription drug, Phenazopyridine hydrochloride (Pyridium®), will help relieve pain and bladder spasms. It also turns urine and other body fluids reddish-orange; so don't wear contacts or expensive underclothes while taking it. Drink lots of fluid, especially cranberry juice if available.

KIDNEY INFECTION (PYELONEPHRITIS)

Signs and Symptoms
Symptoms may include those for bladder infection with the addition of back pain, fever, chills, nausea or vomiting.

Treatment
1) Initially the same as for bladder infections.
2) Evacuate the victim for medical care as soon as possible.

GYNECOLOGICAL EMERGENCIES
VAGINAL BLEEDING
Female travelers may experience a change in their menstrual cycle due to stress. It is important to differentiate irregular vaginal bleeding or cessation of vaginal bleeding from pregnancy. If there is any chance that you may be pregnant, seek medical help.

Any abnormal bleeding or abdominal pain accompanied by vaginal bleeding that is not associated with a normal menstrual period should be evaluated by a physician immediately. An ectopic or tubal pregnancy should be suspected if a menstrual period has been missed and vaginal bleeding and pelvic cramps develop. The condition can rapidly become life-threatening if not treated.

INFECTIONS
Pelvic pain associated with fever, chills, nausea, vomiting, and weakness may indicate a pelvic infection. There may also be a yellow-green discharge. If immediate medical care is not available, the victim should be started on antibiotics

right away (tetracycline 500 mg four times a day or doxycycline 100 mg twice a day and metronidazole [Flagyl®] 250 mg three times a day).

If a vaginal discharge is white and creamy (like cottage cheese) and is associated with vaginal or vulvar itching and burning or pain on urination, it is usually vaginitis or a yeast infection. This can be treated with fluconazole (Diflucan®) 150 mg taken orally or miconazole (Monistat®) or clotrimazole (Gyne-Lotrimin®) vaginal tablets (seven days) or cream (14 days). If none of these drugs is available, a vinegar douche can be helpful, as is airing the vaginal area and switching to cotton underwear or none at all. If the discharge is frothy, white-gray, and accompanied by abdominal pain and fever, it is often due to trichomoniasis. Treat with metronidazole (Flagyl®) 250 mg three times a day for five to seven days.

VOMITING

Treatment

Drink small but frequent amounts of a clear liquid, such as soup, 7-Up®, or half-strength Gatorade®. Avoid drinking too much too soon; the stomach becomes distended, resulting in more vomiting. Avoid solid food until the vomiting has stopped.

WHEN TO WORRY

Vomiting

Obtain professional medical care immediately if vomiting is associated with any of the following:
- Head or abdominal trauma;
- Severe lethargy or confusion;
- Severe abdominal pain or distention;
- If there is blood in the vomit or it has a coffee ground appearance;
- Fever higher than 101 degrees;
- Vomiting alone that continues for longer than 24 hours.

DIARRHEA

Diarrhea is an increase in the frequency and looseness of stools. Causes of diarrhea include viruses, bacteria, parasites such as Giardia or Cryptosporidium, food allergies, inflammatory bowel disease, and anxiety.

A major concern with diarrhea is the amount of fluid loss or dehydration that results. The degree of dehydration can be estimated from certain signs and symptoms:

- **Mild Dehydration** (3% to 5% weight loss)
  Thirst; tacky mucous membranes (lips, mouth); normal pulse; dark urine.
- **Moderate Dehydration** (5% to 10% weight loss)
  Thirst; dry mucous membranes; sunken eyes; small volume of dark urine; rapid and weak pulse.
- **Severe Dehydration** (greater than 10% weight loss)
  Drowsiness or lethargy; very dry mucous membranes; sunken eyes; no urine; no tears; shock (rapid pulse or one that is thready or difficult to feel).

GENERAL TREATMENT OF DIARRHEA
1) Replace Fluids and Electrolytes

Oral rehydration with water and oral rehydration salts (ORS) is the most important treatment for diarrhea illnesses in the backcountry. The fluids and electrolytes lost from diarrhea can be potentially fatal in children and devastating in adults. The body has the ability to absorb the water and electrolytes given orally, even during a severe bout of diarrhea. Diarrhea fluid contains sodium chloride (salt), potassium, and bicarbonate, so simply drinking plain water is inadequate replacement. Many sport drinks sold commercially are not ideal for replacement of diarrhea losses: the high concentration of sugar may increase fluid loss and the electrolyte contents may not be optimal. Gatorade® can be used, but should be diluted to half-strength with water.

The World Health Organization recommends oral rehydration solutions that contain the following combination of electrolytes added to one liter of water: sodium chloride 3.5 g.; potassium chloride 1.5 g.; glucose 20 g., and sodium bicarbonate 2.5 g.

WHEN TO WORRY

Diarrhea
Obtain medical assistance if diarrhea is accompanied by any of the following:
  • Blood or mucus in the stool;
  • A fever greater than 101 degrees;
  • Severe abdominal pain or distention;
  • Moderate to Severe dehydration;
  • Diarrhea lasting longer than three days.

ORS packets can be purchased commercially from *Adventure Medical Kits (800) 324-3517*, or improvised (see below).

Mildly or moderately dehydrated adults should drink between four to six liters of oral rehydration solutions in the first four to six hours. Children can be given eight ounces of ORS every hour. Severe dehydration usually requires evacuation to a medical facility and intravenous fluids.

Rice, bananas, and potatoes are good supplements to oral rehydration solutions. Fats, dairy products, caffeine, and alcohol should be avoided. Avoid drinking full-strength juices as a rehydration solution. Juices usually have three to five times the recommended concentration of sugar and can worsen the diarrhea.

2) Antimotility Drugs

If the victim does not have bloody diarrhea or a fever greater than 101 degrees, loperamide (Imodium®) can be taken orally to reduce cramping and diarrhea. The dose for adults is 4 mg initially, followed by 2 mg after each loose bowel movement up to a maximum of 14 mg per day. Imodium® is preferred over Lomotil® because it has fewer potential side effects. Imodium® should not be given to children. Pepto-Bismol® or Kaopectate® are other commonly used antimotility drugs and may be helpful.

3) Antibiotics
Antibiotics are recommended if the diarrhea is accompanied by fever (101 F. or greater), if there is pus or blood in the stool, if the victim has signs and symptoms of Giardiasis (see below), or if the victim is traveling in a third-world or underdeveloped country (see Traveler's Diarrhea).

'WEISS ADVICE'

[IMPROVISED TECHNIQUE]

Rehydration Solutions
Add one teaspoon table salt, four teaspoons cream of tartar (potassium bicarbonate), one-half teaspoon baking soda, and four tablespoons sugar to one liter (quart) of drinking water.

OR

Alternate drinking two separate solutions prepared in the following manner:
   1) Eight ounces (250 ml) fruit juice, one-half teaspoon of honey or corn syrup and one pinch of salt;
   2) Eight ounces (250 ml) water and one-fourth teaspoon baking soda.

GIARDIA
Giardia is a hardy parasite that can thrive even in very cold water. Just one glass of contaminated water in the backcountry is enough to produce illness. Symptoms of Giardia are usually delayed for seven to 10 days after drinking contaminated water and may last two months or longer if the infection is not treated.

Signs and Symptoms
1) Onset is usually gradual with two to five loose or mushy stools per day.
2) Stools are foul-smelling and contain mucous.
3) The victim usually experiences a rumbling or gurgling feeling in his stomach, has foul-smelling gas, cramping abdominal pain, nausea and burps that taste like rotten eggs.
4) General malaise and weight loss can occur.

Treatment

Nitazoxanide (Alinia®), a prescription medication, is now approved by the FDA for the treatment of Giardia and has a better cure rate than the older medication, metronidazole (Flagyl®). The adult dose is 500 mg twice a day for three days. The dose in children is 100 mg twice a day for three days. The adult dose of metronidazole is 250 mg three times a day for seven days. In Asia and South America, Tinidazole (Tiniba®) is often used and can be taken as a single 2-gram dose to cure the infection.

CRYPTOSPORIDIOSIS (CRYPTO)

Cryptosporidium is a microscopic parasite similar to Giardia that lives in the feces of infected humans and animals. It is found in nearly all surface waters that have been tested nationwide. In 1995, more than 45 million Americans drank water from sources that contained Crypto, and in Milwaukee in 1993, it produced the largest outbreak of waterborne diarrhea in United States history.

Cryptosporidium is a resilient parasite. It is not killed by chlorine or iodine at concentrations normally used to disinfect drinking water, and can slip through many water filters. The parasite is between two and five microns in size. As a result, filters must be able to remove particles smaller than two microns to be effective in eliminating Crypto from the water supply. Fortunately, the bug is vulnerable to heat and can be killed simply by bringing water to full boil.

Signs and Symptoms

In most healthy people, Cryptosporidium causes abdominal cramps, low-grade fever, nausea, vomiting, and diarrhea, which can result in dehydration. Symptoms usually begin two to seven days after drinking contaminated water, and can last for up two to three weeks before resolving on its own. For people with AIDS, on chemotherapy, or who have a weakened immune system, Crypto may last for months and can be fatal.

Treatment

Nitazoxanide (Alinia®) a prescription medication, is now approved by the FDA for the treatment of Cryptosporidium. The adult dose is 500 mg twice a day for three days. Imodium® may help decrease fluid loss and intestinal cramping.

TRAVELER'S DIARRHEA

Traveler's Diarrhea refers to diarrhea that occurs in the context of foreign travel. It usually occurs when people visit underdeveloped or third-world countries.

Prevention

Traveler's Diarrhea is usually caused by bacteria and afflicts almost half of all visitors to underdeveloped countries. It is acquired through ingestion of contaminated food or water. Watching what you eat and drink may help but does not guarantee that you will not get sick. A person traveling should avoid drinking untreated tap water or drinks with ice cubes. Bottled and carbonated drinks are generally safe. Custards, salads, salsas, reheated food, milk, and unpeeled fruits and vegetables should be avoided. Disinfect tap water used for brushing teeth.

Antibiotics are not recommended for prevention, but are reserved for treatment if sickness occurs. Pepto-Bismol® (bismuth subsalicylate) is effective in preventing diarrhea in about 60 percent of travelers, but must be taken in large quantities. Four tablespoons four times a day, or two tablets four times a day, are needed. Unfortunately, this equates to a large amount of aspirin and can give some people stomach problems.

Signs and Symptoms

Symptoms usually begin abruptly two to three days after arrival. The diarrhea can be watery or soft, and there can be cramps, nausea, vomiting, malaise and fever.

Treatment

1) See General Treatment of Diarrhea above.
2) Antibiotics are effective for treating most cases of Traveler's Diarrhea. The best antibiotics are ciprofloxacin (Cipro®) 500 mg twice a day for two to three days or

azithromycin (Zithromax®) 250 mg once a day for two to three days. Cipro® is not approved for use in children and may cause joint pains. A single dose of Ciprofloxacin 750 mg or azithromycin 1000 mg is also effective. It is well worth a visit to your physician for a prescription before your trip.

CONSTIPATION

Constipation (difficult bowel movements with hard stools) is a common problem when traveling in the wilderness, due to disruption of normal habits. Constipation is easier to prevent than to treat. Drinking fluids to stay well hydrated, and adjusting the diet to include fruit, vegetables, and whole grains are helpful. If one is still constipated, a stool softener can be used (mineral oil, Metamucil®), with or without a gentle laxative such as prune juice or Milk of Magnesia®. When no stool has been passed for five to 10 days due to constipation, the stool may have to be removed from the rectum using a gloved finger or enema. This should be done carefully to prevent injury to the anus and walls of the rectum.

HEMORRHOIDS

Hemorrhoids are enlarged veins found both outside and inside the anal opening. They can cause minor itching, severe pain, and bleeding. The best way to prevent hemorrhoids is to prevent constipation (see above).

Treatment

Hemorrhoids can be treated topically with over-the-counter preparations such as Anusol® or Preparation H®. Any ointment with hydrocortisone will also be effective. Tucks® hemorrhoidal pads with witch hazel are excellent for hemorrhoids and also help to soothe poison ivy/oak rashes.

ALLERGIC EMERGENCIES

Allergic reactions can occur as a result of insect stings, food allergies, medications, exposure to animals, severe asthma, and other unknown reasons. Allergic reactions to insect stings are usually from the sting of a bee, wasp, hornet, yellow jacket, or from the bite of a fire ant. The most severe form of an allergic reaction is anaphylactic shock, which can be life-threatening within minutes after contact with the substance to which the individual is allergic.

SEVERE ALLERGIC EMERGENCIES (ANAPHYLACTIC SHOCK)

The victim may develop hives (red, raised skin welts), wheezing, chest tightness, shortness of breath, and a drop in blood pressure leading to dizziness, lightheadedness and fainting. The soft tissues of the throat, larynx or trachea may swell, making it difficult or impossible for the person to swallow or breathe.

Treatment

The treatment for anaphylactic shock is epinephrine (adrenaline), and it needs to be given in the field.

People allergic to bee stings or with other serious allergies should carry injectable epinephrine with them at all times.

Epinephrine is available in a spring-loaded injectable cartridge called the Epi E•Z Pen® (Center Laboratories). This allows for self-administration of the medicine without dealing with a needle and syringe. The device contains 2 ml of epinephrine 1:1000 USP in a disposable push-button, spring-activated cartridge with a concealed needle. It will deliver a single dose of 0.3 mg epinephrine intramuscularly. For children who weigh less than 66 lbs., there is the Epi E•Z Pen®Jr, which contains half the dose of the adult injection. Instructions for use accompany the kits. Obtaining epinephrine requires a prescription from your doctor.

After administering epinephrine, give the victim oral diphenhydramine (Benadryl®25 to 50 mg). Diphenhydramine is an antihistamine and may lessen the allergic reaction.

After treatment, transport the victim to a medical facility immediately, as an anaphylactic reaction can recur once the epinephrine wears off.

MILD ALLERGIC REACTIONS

All allergic reactions are not life-threatening. Often one may only develop hives (red, raised skin welts) and itching without wheezing or other breathing problems.

Treatment

These reactions may be managed with an antihistamine such as diphenhydramine (Benadryl®). The adult dose is 25 to 50 mg every four to six hours. The major side effect of this medication is drowsiness.

ASTHMA

Asthma, a respiratory disease involving the bronchial tubes in the lung, can be life-threatening, especially in children. Many factors can predispose a susceptible individual to an attack, including pollen, animal hair, certain foods, upper respiratory infections, emotional stress, exercise, or exposure to cold air. During an acute attack, the muscles around the small breathing tubes in the lungs tighten or constrict, causing wheezing, coughing, and the sensation of not being able to get enough air. Other symptoms of a severe attack include bluish tinge to the lips and fingers, rapid heartbeat, gasping for air, and confusion.

Treatment

Breathing medications which contain bronchodilators (albuterol) are most helpful during an attack. If the attack is severe, epinephrine from an Epi E•Z Pen® may be administered as described above. Other useful medications include diphenhydramine (Benadryl®50 mg.), and corticosteroids (prednisone 2 mg/kg). The victim should be evacuated to a medical facility as soon as possible.

INSECT BITES AND STINGS

Venom from insects can produce severe allergic reactions and lead to life-threatening anaphylactic shock (See page 119).

More commonly, insect bites and stings are painful and produce local reactions (redness, swelling) at the site.

General Treatment
- Ice or cold packs will help alleviate local pain and swelling.
- Sting relief swabs may help relieve pain when applied topically.
- Oral antihistamines, such as diphenhydramine (Benadryl®25 to 50 mg every four hours) are helpful in relieving the itching, rash, and swelling associated with many insect bites and stings.
- The principles of wound care discussed on page 86 apply to bites and stings as well. Any bite or sting can become infected and should therefore be examined at regular intervals for progressive redness, swelling, pain, or pus drainage.
- Infectious diseases can be spread by insect bites, especially in tropical and third-world countries. Wearing protective clothing and applying insect repellents containing DEET are important preventive measures.

BEE STINGS
Honey bees leave a stinger and venom sac in the victim after a sting. Hornets, yellow jackets, bumblebees, and wasps do not leave a stinger and may puncture a victim repeatedly. Pain is immediate and may be accompanied by swelling, redness, and warmth at the site.

Treatment:
1. If anaphylactic shock occurs, it must be treated immediately with epinephrine and antihistamines (See page 119).
2. After a honey bee sting, first remove the stinger and venom sac as quickly as possible. Even with the rest of the bee gone, the venom sac can still continue to pump

venom into your skin. Do not hesitate or fumble for a
pocket knife or credit card to scrape the stinger out of
the skin. It is better to grab the stinger and yank it out
quickly than worry about pinching or squeezing more
venom from the sac.
3. Apply ice or cold water to the sting site.
4. Anesthetic sprays, swabs and creams may help relieve
pain.
5. For adults, administer 25 to 50 mg diphenhydramine
(Benadryl®) for progressive itching, swelling, or redness.

'WEISS ADVICE'

[IMPROVISED TECHNIQUE]

Taking the sting out of bee & wasp venom

For bee venom (which is acid), apply a paste of baking soda
and water. For wasp venom (which is alkaline), apply vinegar,
lemon juice, or other acidic substance. Meat tenderizer applied
locally to the sting site may also be effective in denaturing the
venom and relieving pain and inflammation.

BLACK WIDOW SPIDER BITES
(LACTRODECTUS MACTANS)

Black widow spiders are black with a red hourglass mark
on the underside of the abdomen and are about 5/8 inch
long. They like to hang out in wood piles, stone walls, and
outhouses. They generally are nocturnal.

Signs and Symptoms

Their bite feels like a sharp pinprick but sometimes may
go unnoticed. Within one hour, the victim may develop a
tingling and numbing sensation in the palms of the hands and
bottoms of the feet, along with muscle cramps, particularly
in the abdomen (stomach) and back. In severe cases, the
stomach muscles may become rigid and board-like. Sweating
and vomiting are common and the victim may complain of
headache and weakness. High blood pressure and seizures
can occur.

Treatment

Most people will recover in eight to 12 hours without treatment. Small children and elderly victims, however, may have severe reactions, occasionally leading to death.

1. Apply ice packs to the bite to relieve pain.
2. Transport the victim to a medical facility as soon as possible.
3. Muscle relaxers such as Valium® Robaxin® or Flexaril® will help relieve muscle spasms.
4. A specific antidote is available for those suffering severe symptoms.

BROWN RECLUSE SPIDER BITE
(LOXASCELES RECLUSA)

The brown recluse spider is found most commonly in the South and southern Midwest parts of the United States. The spider is brownish, with a body length of 10 mm. (just under 1/2 inch). A characteristic dark, violin-shaped marking is found on the top of the upper section of the body.

Signs and Symptoms

The bite sensation is initially mild, producing the same degree of pain as that of an ant sting. The stinging subsides over six to eight hours and is replaced by aching and itching at the bite site. Within one to five hours, a painful red blister appears, surrounded by a bull's eye of whitish-blue discoloration. Over the next 10 to 14 days the blister ruptures and a gradually enlarging ulcer crater develops, with further destruction of tissue. Fever, chills, weakness, nausea, and vomiting may develop within 24 to 48 hours of the bite.

Treatment

1) Apply ice or cold compresses to the wound for pain relief.
2) If the blister has ruptured, apply a topical antibiotic ointment to the wound and cover with a nonadherent sterile dressing and bandage.
3) The victim should obtain medical care as soon as possible. An antivenin is now available which, when used early, can prevent loss of tissue and scarring.

TARANTULA BITE

Tarantulas are large, slow spiders capable of inflicting a painful bite that can sometimes become infected.

Treatment
1. Apply ice for pain relief.
2. Elevate and immobilize the bitten extremity to reduce pain.
3. Apply an antibiotic ointment to the site.
4. Take Motrin® or Tylenol® for pain, and antihistamines for itching

SCORPION STING

Scorpions are nocturnal and hide during the day under bark, in rocky crevices, or in the sand. Stings can be avoided by shaking out your shoes and clothes in the morning before dressing, not walking barefoot after dark, and by looking before picking up rocks or wood under which scorpions hide during the day.

Most North American scorpion stings produce only localized pain and swelling. The venom is injected by the stinger in the scorpion's tail. The pain of a nonlethal species is similar to that of a wasp or hornet, and the treatment is similar. Severe allergic reactions to scorpion stings are rare.

The potentially lethal scorpion found in the United States is Centuroides sculpturatus, also known as the bark scorpion, from its habit of hiding beneath loose and fallen pieces of tree bark. It is found in the desert areas of the southwestern United States (Arizona, New Mexico, California, and Texas) and northern Mexico. It is usually small (2 to 4 centimeters in length), straw-yellow colored, with long slender pincers as opposed to bulky and lobster-like. The venom contains neurotoxins that can be lethal, but usually only in infants or small children.

The bark scorpion's sting causes immediate pain, which is worsened by tapping lightly over the bite site. Other symptoms include restlessness, muscle twitching which can sometimes look like a seizure, blurred vision, roving eye movements, trouble swallowing, drooling, slurred speech, numbness and tingling around the mouth, feet and hands, and difficulty breathing.

Treatment
1. Place a piece of ice over the sting area to reduce pain.
2. Seek professional medical care as soon as possible, as an antivenin is available in the areas where lethal scorpions live.

FIRE ANT BITE (SOLENOPSIS INVICTA)
Fire ants are found in the southeastern states, Texas, and parts of California. They range in color from dull yellow to red or black. The ants are tenacious and swarm and sting their victim repeatedly.

Signs and Symptoms
Initially, there develops a cluster of small, painful and itchy blisters. These usually evolve into small pustules (boils) within 24 hours. The skin over the pustule will slough away in two to three days, after which the sores heal. Some victims develop a severe reaction characterized by large, red, swollen welts that are very itchy. About one percent of stings are followed by severe allergic reactions.

Treatment
1. Apply ice or cold packs to the area.
2. Administer Motrin® or Tylenol® with codeine for pain.
3. The rash and itching can be treated with antihistamines such as Benadryl 25 to 50 mg every four to six hours. Topical steroid creams such as hydrocortisone or triamcinalone may also help to reduce the itching. In severe cases, a prescription for an oral steroid (prednisone) can be obtained from your physician, which will dramatically reduce itching.

CATERPILLARS
The pus caterpillar or woolly slug (Megalopyge opercularis) found in the southern United States has venomous bristles that inflict a painful sting. Contact with one causes instant pain, followed by redness and swelling at the site. Symptoms usually subside within 24 hours. In rare cases, nausea, headache, fever, vomiting, and shock may occur.

Treatment
1. Pat the skin with a piece of adhesive tape to remove any remaining bristles.
2. Apply hydrocortisone cream to the site to reduce itching, or take an oral antihistamine such as Benadryl®.

TICKS
Ticks are brushed onto people who pass close by. Once a tick lands on a person, it clings to hair or clothing and waits for several hours until the individual is at rest. Then it moves to an exposed area, often around the tops of the socks or at the neckline, attaches itself and begins feeding. An anesthetic agent in the tick's saliva usually makes the bite painless. Ticks feed from two hours to several days before dropping off.

Ticks secrete saliva and disease-producing organisms into the victim while feeding. About 100 tick species transmit infections to man. The most infamous are the tiny deer tick (Ixodes scapularis) and black-legged tick (Ixodes pacificus) which spreads Lyme disease and Ehrlichia; the lone star tick, which transmits Rocky Mountain spotted fever; and the dog tick, which transmits Ehrlichia.

Prevention
1. Spray tents, sleeping bags, and clothing with Perme-thrin, an insecticide that kills ticks before they have a chance to get embedded into your skin. Permethrin remains effective on your clothes for up to two weeks, and through several washings. It should not be used directly on the skin.
2. Apply an insect repellent to your skin.
3. Check yourself and your companions for ticks ("tick patrol") at least every four hours when in tick country.
4. Wear long pants that are tucked into the socks.
5. Wear clothing that is light in color, making it easier to spot ticks.

Fig. 59 - Tick removal

How to Remove an Embedded Tick

The tick should be grasped as close to the skin or surface as possible with tweezers, taking care not to crush, squeeze, or puncture the body **(Fig. 59)**. Apply steady, straight upward traction to remove the tick. It may take a couple of minutes to convince the tick to let go. Avoid twisting, as it can break off and leave behind mouth parts. Traditional folk methods for removing ticks such as applying fingernail polish, petrolatum jelly, rubbing alcohol, or a hot match increase the chance that the tick will salivate or regurgitate into the wound, thus spreading infection. After removal, clean the bite site with an antiseptic towelette.

Local Reactions

Tick bites can occasionally produce a painful red and swollen wound at the puncture site, which can take a week or two to heal. The site can also become infected, requiring topical and oral antibiotics. If parts of the tick are left embedded in the skin, a painful nodule develops which then must be removed by surgical excision.

Some ticks carry a neurotoxin in their saliva and on rare occasions a bite can lead to a temporary, or sometimes fatal, paralysis. Paralysis usually occurs only after prolonged attachment (more than five days) and begins in the legs and spreads to the arms and trunk and head. Removal of the tick stops the paralysis and the victim recovers completely within several hours.

LYME DISEASE

Lyme disease is an infection caused by a spirochete, a type of bacteria that invades your body during the bite of an infected tick. Lyme disease is now the most common tick-transmitted infection, with an estimated 5,000 to 15,000 new cases in the United States each year. The majority of people with Lyme disease do not recall the precipitating tick bite.

Lyme disease is most common in the Northeast coastal states (New York, Connecticut, Pennsylvania, New Jersey, and Rhode Island), in the upper Midwest (especially Michigan, Wisconsin, and Minnesota), and on the Pacific Coast in California and Oregon. In areas of the Northeast, 90 percent of the deer ticks are infected with Lyme disease. In the West, only about one to two percent of the ticks are infected.

Signs and Symptoms

Ranging from three days to a month (average of seven days) after the tick bite, 70 percent of infected individuals develop an expanding, circular red rash (erythema migrains). As the rash expands, it partially clears in the center, while the outer borders remain bright red, giving the appearance of a "bull's-eye." The rash can reach a diameter of six inches and may appear anywhere on the skin, unrelated to the bite site, although the thigh, groin and armpits are the most common locations. The rash is warm to the touch and usually described by the victim as itching or burning, but rarely painful. It fades after an average of 28 days without treatment; with antibiotics, the rash resolves after several days.

Flu-like symptoms, with fever, fatigue, headache, and muscle and joint aches, may develop before or with the rash, and last for a few days.

About 20 percent of untreated people develop severe complications within weeks or months after the bite, ranging from heart and neurologic problems to severe attacks of arthritis (pain in the joints).

Treatment

If you develop a red rash after a tick bite in the backcounty, it is best to abort the trip and seek medical attention. The rash will help the physician diagnose Lyme disease and lead to early treatment with antibiotics.

VENOMOUS SNAKE BITES

There are two classes of poisonous snakes in the United States:

- Pit Vipers (rattlesnakes, cottonmouths [water moccasins], and copperheads) have a characteristic triangular head, a deep pit (heat receptor organ) between the eye and nostril, and a catlike, elliptical pupil.
- Elapids (coral snakes) are characterized by their color pattern with red, black, and yellow or white bands encircling the body. The fangs are short — these snakes bite by chewing rather than by striking.

All states except Maine, Hawaii, and Alaska have at least one species of venomous snake. The states with the highest incidence of snakebites are North Carolina, Arkansas, Texas, Mississippi, Louisiana, Arizona, and New Mexico. About 90 percent of snake bites occur between April and October, because snakes are more active in warm months of the year. Your chance of dying from a venomous snakebite in the wilderness is extremely remote — about one in 12 million.

Snakes can strike up to one-half their body length and may bite and not inject venom (dry bite). No poisoning occurs in about 20 to 30 percent of rattlesnake bites, and fewer than 40 percent of coral snake bites result in envenomation.

PIT VIPERS

Signs and Symptoms of Envenomation

- One or more fang marks (rattlesnake bites may leave one, two, or even three fang marks).
- Local, burning pain immediately after the bite.
- Swelling at the site of the bite, usually beginning within five to 20 minutes and spreading slowly over a period of six to 12 hours. The faster the swelling progresses up the arm or leg, the worse the degree of envenomation.
- Bruising (black and blue discoloration) and blister formation at the bite site.
- Numbness and tingling of the lips and face, usually 10 to 60 minutes after the bite.

- Twitching of the muscles around the eyes and mouth.
- Rubbery or metallic taste in the mouth.
- After six to 12 hours, bleeding from the gums and nose may develop and denote a serious envenomation.
- Weakness, sweating, nausea, vomiting and faintness may occur.

Treatment

The definitive treatment for snake venom poisoning is the administration of antivenin. The most important aspect of therapy is to get the victim to a medical facility as quickly as possible.

First Aid

1) Rinse the area around the bite site with water to remove any venom that might remain on the skin.
2) Clean the wound and cover with a sterile dressing.
3) Remove any rings or jewelry.
4) Immobilize the injured part as you would for a fracture, but splint it just below the level of the heart.
5) Transport the victim to the nearest hospital as soon as possible. If you pass by a telephone, stop and notify the hospital that you are bringing in a snakebite victim so they can begin to locate and procure antivenin.
6) It is not necessary to kill the snake and transport it with the victim for identification. If the snake is killed, it should not be directly handled, but should be transported in a closed container. Decapitated snake heads can still produce envenomation
7) Extractor pumps designed to provide suction over a snakebite wound are sold in many camping stores and endorsed by some as a first aid treatment for snakebites. Based on recent scientific evidence, these devices are no longer recommended. A study published in the Annals of Emergency Medicine in 2004 showed that these devices remove an insignificant amount of venom, and may also be harmful to the victim. The best first aid for snakebite is a cell phone (call the hospital that you are going to so that they can procure antivenin) and a car or helicopter to get the victim there as quickly as possible.

***Other First-Aid Treatments
That May Be Beneficial***

Immediately wrapping the entire bitten extremity with a broad elastic bandage (the "Australian Compression and Immobilization Technique") has proven effective in the treatment of elapid and sea snake envenomations only. It is only recommended when the victim appears to have suffered a severe envenomation and is several hours from medical care.

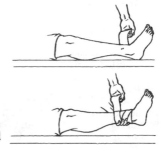

The wrap is started over the bite site and continued upward toward the torso in an even fashion about as tight as one would wrap a sprained ankle

Fig. 60 - Australian wrap for snake envenomation.

(Fig. 60). Monitor the color, pulse and temperature of the hand or foot to make sure that there is adequate circulation. If circulation appears compromised, loosen the wrap. Otherwise the bandage should not be released until after the victim has been brought to a medical facility. The limb should then be immobilized with a well-padded splint.

THINGS NOT TO DO
1) Do not make any incisions in the skin or apply suction with your mouth.
2) Do not apply ice or a tourniquet.
3) Do not shock the victim with a stun gun or electrical current.

CORAL SNAKE

Signs and Symptoms of Envenomation
• Burning pain at the site of the bite.
• Numbness and/or weakness of a bitten arm or leg develops within 90 minutes.
• Twitching, nervousness, drowsiness, increased salivation, and drooling develop within one to three hours.

- Within five to ten hours, the victim develops slurred speech, double vision, difficulty talking and swallowing, and difficulty breathing. The venom may cause total paralysis.

Symptoms may sometimes be delayed by up to 13 hours after the bite.

First Aid

Treatment is the same as for a pit viper bite. Early use of the pressure immobilization technique is highly recommended because it is both effective and safe (coral snake venom does not produce any local tissue destruction).

VENOMOUS LIZARDS

The Gila monster and Mexican beaded lizard are found only in the Great Sonoran Desert area in southern Arizona and northwestern Mexico. Both possess venom glands and grooved teeth capable of envenomating humans. Not all bites result in envenomation, since the lizard may only nip the victim, or not expel any venom during a bite.

Gila monsters may hang on tenaciously during a bite, and pliers or a sharp knife may be required to loosen the grip of its jaws.

Signs and Symptoms of Envenomation

1) Pain and severe burning are felt at the wound site within five minutes and may radiate up the extremity. Intense pain may last from three to five hours and then subside after eight hours.
2) Swelling occurs at the wound site, usually within 15 minutes, and progresses slowly up the extremity. Blue discoloration may appear around the wound.

First Aid

1) Clean the wound thoroughly as you would for any laceration (See page 87).
2) Inspect the wound and remove any shed or broken teeth.
3) Immobilize and elevate the extremity.
4) Obtain medical care as soon as possible.

ANIMAL BITES

Human or animal bites often become infected and can transmit diseases, such as rabies. Cat bites are especially prone to infection.

General Treatment

1) Clean the wound vigorously as described in Wound Care (page 87).
2) The best antiseptic for bite wounds is benzalkonium chloride, because it helps to kill the rabies virus.
3) Never close an animal bite with sutures or tape. Pack the wound with saline-moistened gauze pads and cover with another dressing and bandage. Change the dressing daily.
4) Seek medical attention as soon as possible.

RABIES

Although rabies is uncommon (there have been only 18 human deaths from rabies in the past 15 years), if not treated right away, it will kill 100 percent of its victims. In the United States, raccoons, skunks, and bats account for 96 percent of rabies cases, while foxes and coyotes make up most of the remaining cases. Any unprovoked attack by one of these animals should be considered an attack by a rabid animal.

Infection can occur even if you aren't bitten. The lick of an animal infected with rabies can transmit the disease if the saliva contacts an open wound or mucous membrane. There are even case reports of victims becoming infected with rabies after breathing the virus in bat-ridden caves. Squirrels, rats, mice, gerbils, chipmunks, and opossums have not been found to transmit rabies.

The rabies virus is transmitted to humans in the saliva of infected animals and attaches itself to nerves at the bite site. It then moves along the nerves to the brain. Because the virus causes no reaction until it reaches the brain, you don't know you're infected until it's too late. Once the virus has invaded the brain and symptoms develop, treatment is no longer effective and death is inevitable.

The average time between the bite and the appearance of symptoms is 30 days. A bite on a leg allows more time for treatment than a bite on an arm, because the virus has farther to travel to reach the brain. Bites about the face are particularly dangerous and must be treated immediately.

Signs and Symptoms

The initial symptoms are nonspecific and include malaise, fatigue, anxiety, agitation, irritability, insomnia, fever, headache, nausea, vomiting and sore throat. After two to 10 more days, the victim may become aggressive, hyperactive and irrational and develop seizures and hallucinations.

Treatment

1) Aggressively swab the wound thoroughly with benzalkonium chloride. If nothing else is available, scrub the wound vigorously with soap and water. Then irrigate the wound with lots of water.
2) If the biting animal can be safely captured, it should be observed for signs of rabies. If it's killed, the brain tissue can be tested for the virus.
3) The victim should seek the assistance of a physician as soon as possible. The doctor will determine the need for rabies vaccination (five shots in the arm) and the administration of anti rabies serum.

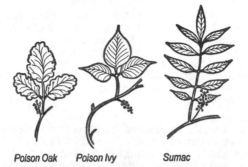

Poison Oak   Poison Ivy   Sumac

POISON IVY, OAK, AND SUMAC

Contact with poison ivy, oak, or sumac can cause an extremely itchy rash. The risk of developing a rash after exposure to these plants increases with each exposure. Your degree of sensitivity can change drastically from one exposure to the next. You may have a minor rash one year, and then be incapacitated by a major breakout the next year.

The offending resin is present in the plants year-round, even when they are only sticks or vines without leaves in the winter. In general, poison ivy grows east of the Rockies, poison oak grows west, and poison sumac grows best in the southeastern United States. They do not grow in Alaska and Hawaii, nor do they survive well above 4,000 feet, in deserts, or in rainforests.

The leaflets on poison ivy and oak grow in clusters of three leading to the saying, "leaflets three, let them be." Poison sumac leaflets grow in groups of seven to 13. The poison ivy vine can wind around a tree trunk or stretch across the ground. Poison oak is a low-growing shrub or woody vine, and poison sumac resembles a shrub or small tree.

The FDA has approved an over-the-counter cream, Ivy Block, (Enviroderm, Louisville, Ky.) that can provide some protection if placed on the skin at least 15 minutes before possible exposure to the plant. The cream is of no use if you already have the rash. Do not use on children younger than six years unless directed by a physician.

The plants' sticky resin can stay active on clothing or shoes for many months, however, so contaminated clothing should be handled carefully and laundered immediately.

The resin binds to skin within 30 minutes. After that length of time it cannot be washed off with soap and water. Some solvents such as Tecnu Poison Oak-n-Ivy Cleanser® may be able to remove the oil from the skin, even when used several hours after exposure.

Signs and Symptoms

The rash may take from a few hours to days to develop and starts as red, itchy bumps, followed by blisters that may become crusted. It can be streaky or patchy, and "itches like crazy." It appears first where the concentration of resin was strongest, and emerges over time on other areas of the body where it was less concentrated. This leads to the misconception that the oozing fluid from the skin spreads the rash. The rash cannot be spread by scratching after you have washed the original oil from the skin. Scratching is still discouraged because it can produce a secondary skin infection and actually increase itching.

Treatment

- If left untreated, the rash will generally clear in about two weeks.
- Over-the-counter steroid creams (hydrocortisone cream 1%) and calamine lotion are not very effective.
- Cool, wet compresses made with Domeboro® astringent solution may provide some relief from the itching.
- Oral antihistamines such as Benadryl® 25 to 50 mg every four to six hours will help relieve some of the itching, but they also make you drowsy.
- For a widespread rash, or one involving the face or genitals, a physician can prescribe strong corticosteroid drugs such as prednisone, which can be taken orally or via injection. It takes about 12 hours for the drug to work, but once it does, the relief is dramatic. Side effects from a two-week course of prednisone are generally mild and worth the benefit.

ALTITUDE ILLNESS
(MOUNTAIN SICKNESS)

It is rare to experience altitude illness below 6,000 feet. Moderate altitude is between 8,000 and 12,000 feet (2,400 and 3,600 meters), High altitude is between 12,000 and 18,000 feet (3,600 and 5,400 meters), and extreme altitude is over 18,000 feet (5,400 meters).

High altitude illness is a direct result of the reduced barometric pressure and concentration of oxygen in the air at high elevations. Lower pressure makes the air less dense, so your body gets fewer oxygen molecules with every breath.

Prevention

Graded ascent is the best and safest method of preventing altitude illness. Avoid abrupt ascent to sleeping altitudes greater than 10,000 feet (3,000 meters), and average no more than 1,000 feet (300 meters) of elevation gain per day above 10,000 feet. Day trips to a higher altitude, with a return to lower altitude for sleep, will aid acclimatization. Eat foods that are high in carbohydrates and low in fat, and stay well hydrated.

WHEN TO WORRY

Descend Quickly When...

Progression of one's symptoms despite rest at the same altitude, or the loss of coordination, mandate immediate descent to a lower altitude (2,000 to 3,000 feet lower). Do not wait for morning to begin descent. An individual who might have been able to walk down under his own power with the aid of a head lamp can easily become a litter case in just 12 hours.

The single most useful sign for recognizing the progression of altitude illness from mild to severe is loss of coordination. The victim tends to stagger, has trouble with balance, and is unable to walk a straight line heel to toe, as if he were drunk.

Never allow a victim to descend alone. Always have a healthy person accompany the individual.

Acetazolamide (Diamox®) is a prescription medication that may help prevent altitude illness when used in conjunction with graded ascent. Diamox works by increasing the respiratory rate, which is especially beneficial while you're asleep. It is also a diuretic (increases urination) and may predispose you to dehydration, so drink lots of fluids and be prepared for the inconvenience of getting up in the night to pee. The dose for prevention is 125 mg the morning before you arrive at altitude, again that evening and then twice a day while you are ascending. Continue taking Diamox for at least 48 hours after reaching your maximum altitude.

CAUTION: Before using Diamox, consult a physician. It can cause an allergic reaction in susceptible individuals and produce numbness and tingling in the hands and feet. Diamox will also ruin the taste of beer, cola and other carbonated beverages.

Ginkgo biloba is an herbal extract that may mitigate the effects of acute mountain sickness (AMS). In three recent studies, it reduced AMS from 35 to 100%. The dose is 100 mg twice a day starting two to three days before and while at altitude. It is not effective for preventing or treating high-altitude pulmonary or cerebral edema.

Altitude illness can be divided into mild and severe forms.

MILD ALTITUDE ILLNESS (ACUTE MOUNTAIN SICKNESS)

Signs and Symptoms

Acute mountain sickness (AMS) is common in travelers who ascend rapidly to altitudes above 7,000 feet. The typical sufferer experiences a headache, difficulty sleeping, loss of appetite, and nausea. Swelling of the face and hands may be an early sign. Children are generally more susceptible than adults.

Sleep is often fitful, with frequent awakenings and an irregular pattern of breathing characterized by periods of rapid breathing alternating with periods of no breathing.

Treatment
1) When mild symptoms develop, one should not go any higher in altitude until the symptoms have completely resolved. Watch the victim closely for progression of illness to more severe forms. Usually, within one or two days, the victim will feel better and can then travel to higher altitudes with caution. Symptoms will improve more rapidly simply by going down a few thousand feet.
2) Administer acetaminophen (Tylenol®) 650 to 1000 mg or ibuprofen (Motrin®) 400 to 600 mg for headache.
3) Consider administering acetazolamide (Diamox®) at a treatment dose of 250 mg twice a day (See Diamox above).
4) Minimize exertion.
5) Avoid sleeping pills.

SEVERE ALTITUDE ILLNESS
HIGH ALTITUDE CEREBRAL EDEMA (HACE)

Signs and Symptoms
A victim may have one or more of the following:
1) Severe headache unrelieved by Tylenol® or Motrin®;
2) Vomiting;
3) Loss of coordination;
4) Severe lassitude;
5) Confusion, inappropriate behavior, hallucinations, stupor or coma;
6) Transient blindness, partial paralysis or loss of sensation on one side of the body may occur;
7) Seizures.

Treatment
1) IMMEDIATE DESCENT of at least 3,000 feet (1,000 meters), or until the victim shows signs of considerable improvement, is the most important treatment. Do not wait to see if the victim gets worse or improves. Waiting could prove to be fatal.
2) Administer acetazolamide (Diamox®) 250 mg twice a day.

3) Administer dexamethasone (Decadron®) 8 mg followed by 4 mg every six hours if available.
4) Administer oxygen, if available.
5) When descent is not immediately possible, placing the victim in a portable hyperbaric chamber (Gamow Bag) may be helpful in mitigating the effects of HACE or HAPE. When zippered shut with the victim inside, this nylon bag is pressurized with a foot pump, resulting in a significant decrease in altitude for the victim. The bag takes approximately two minutes to inflate and is labor intensive; it requires 10 to 15 pumps per minute to maintain pressure and to flush out carbon dioxide. The Gamow Bag should not be used as a substitute for descent; it should be used when descent is not possible due to darkness, injury, or lack of manpower to carry a victim to a lower altitude.

The Golden Rules of Altitude Illness

1) Above 8,000 feet, headache, nausea, shortness of breath, and vomiting should be considered to be altitude illness until proven otherwise.
2) No one with mild symptoms of altitude illness should ascend any higher until symptoms have resolved.
3) Anyone with worsening symptoms or severe symptoms of altitude illness should descend immediately to a lower altitude.

HIGH ALTITUDE PULMONARY EDEMA (HAPE)
HAPE usually begins within the first two to four days of ascent to higher altitudes, most commonly on the second night.

Signs and Symptoms
A victim may have one or more of the following:
1) Initially, the victim will notice marked breathlessness with minor exertion and develop a dry, hacking cough.
2) As fluid collects in the lungs, the victim develops increasing shortness of breath, even while resting, and a cough that may produce frothy sputum.

3) The victim looks anxious, is restless, and has a rapid, bounding pulse.
4) Cyanosis (a bluish color of the lips and nails indicating poor oxygenation of the blood) may be present.

Treatment
1) IMMEDIATE DESCENT of at least 3,000 feet (1,000 meters), or until the victim shows signs of considerable improvement, is the most important treatment. Do not wait. Waiting could prove to be fatal.
2) Administer oxygen, four to six liters per minute, if available.
3) The prescription drug, nifedipine (Procardia®) may be helpful for HAPE. The dose is 10 to 20 mg every eight hours.
4) The use of the Gamow Bag, as described above, may be beneficial when the victim cannot be immediately evacuated to a lower altitude.

FROSTNIP, FROSTBITE & IMMERSION FOOT

Prevention
Frostbite occurs in cold and windy weather conditions. Even if the temperature outdoors is not very cold, high winds can reduce the effective temperature to a dangerously low level. The chilling effect of air at 20 degrees F. moving at 40 miles an hour is the same as 20-below-zero air on a still day.

On long trips it is important to drink often to prevent dehydration and to eat often to provide fuel for your body to generate heat. If the body is cold and dehydrated, it will shunt blood away from the skin, predisposing you to frost-bite.

Other things that predispose one to frostbite and that should be avoided are smoking, tight restrictive clothing and shoes, and contact of bare flesh with cold metal. Individuals with diabetes, known sensitivity to cold, and poor circulation are more likely to suffer frostbite.

FROSTNIP

Frostnip (also called superficial frostbite) is an early cold injury to the skin and does not usually lead to permanent damage. It may progress to deeper frostbite if left untreated. It is usually characterized by numbness of the involved area. Common locations are the fingers, toes, nose, and earlobes. The affected parts will initially appear red and then turn pale or whitish. Frostnipped parts are still soft and pliable to the touch.

Treatment

1) Frostnipped areas should be rewarmed immediately to prevent the progression to frostbite. Place your fingers in your own armpit or groin, and leave them there until they are warm and no longer numb. Place your bared feet onto the warm stomach of a companion.

2) Chemical heat packs are also beneficial, but take care not to burn the skin.

FROSTBITE

Frostbite is freezing of the skin and usually indicates that some degree of permanent damage has occurred. It is recognized by skin that is white and waxy in appearance. The frostbitten part feels hard like a piece of wood.

Treatment

The best treatment for frostbite is rapid rewarming in warm water as soon as the victim can be maintained in a warm environment. Rapid rewarming is preferable to slow rewarming, because the damage to tissue occurs during the actual freezing and thawing phases. If possible, avoid rewarming the frostbitten area if there is a danger of refreezing. Walking on frozen feet to shelter is much less damaging than walking on feet that have been thawed. Allowing the feet to refreeze again after thawing is the worst possible scenario.

1) Rapidly rewarm frozen extremities in water at a temperature of 104 to 106 degrees F. Circulate the water to keep the involved part in contact with the warmest water, and avoid rubbing or massaging the skin. Keep checking the water temperature, as it will cool quickly.

Add more hot water if needed. Remove the extremity from the water before adding more hot water. Thawing in warm water usually requires 30 to 45 minutes of immersion and can be very painful. If pain medication is available, a dose should be given to the victim before beginning. Thawing is complete when the paleness has turned to a pink or red color and the skin is soft.

2) After thawing, the involved part will be very sensitive to further injury and should be protected. Application of aloe vera gel to the skin has been shown to be beneficial in promoting healing of frostbitten skin.

3) When frostbite is rewarmed, fluid-filled blisters (blebs) may form. If this occurs, remove the loose skin overlying the blister and apply aloe vera or antiseptic ointment.

4) Place small sterile gauze pads between toes or fingers, cover the injury with a nonadherent sterile dressing and loosely wrap the extremity with a bulky bandage.

5) Administer ibuprofen (Motrin®) 600 to 800 mg every 12 hours. Ibuprofen will help relieve pain and may minimize tissue loss.

6) Elevate and splint the affected part.

The depth and degree of the frozen tissue cannot be readily determined by looking at the part. Even terrible-looking limbs often recover if treated well, so reassure the victim and seek professional medical care as soon as possible.

THINGS NOT TO DO

1) Do not rub the affected part with snow. In fact, do not massage, rub, or touch the frozen part at all.

2) Be careful not to use water that is hotter than 106 F, because a burn injury may result.

3) The victim should avoid all types of tobacco. Nicotine markedly reduces blood flow to the fingers and toes.

4) Do not thaw the frozen extremity in front of a fire or stove.

5) Do not let the thawed extremity refreeze.

6) Walking on frostbitten feet or using frostbitten fingers will cause further injury and should be avoided when possible.

IMMERSION FOOT (TRENCHFOOT)

Trenchfoot occurs in response to exposure to nonfreezing cold and wet conditions over a number of days, leading to damage of blood vessels, nerves, skin and sometimes muscle, without complete freezing of tissues.

Signs and Symptoms

1) Numbness and a "pins and needle sensation" may occur in the feet.
2) During the first few hours to days, the feet become very red and swollen and then mottled with dark red to blue splotches.
3) The feet can become extremely painful after rewarming and very sensitive to cold and touch.

Treatment

Keep the feet dry and warm and treat as you would for frostbite, with the exception that rapid rewarming (thawing) is not necessary.

HYPOTHERMIA

Hypothermia is an abnormally low body temperature due to exposure to a cold environment. Core (rectal) temperature down to 90 degrees F (32 degrees centigrade) is considered mild to moderate hypothermia, while temperatures below this indicate profound or severe hypothermia. When the body's temperature falls below 83 degrees, the heart becomes irritable and is prone to lethal irregularities, such as ventricular fibrillation. Death from hypothermia is likely to occur at around 75 to 80 degrees. The lowest recorded core temperature in a surviving adult is 60.8 degrees F. For a child, it is 57 degrees F.

Although few people freeze to death in the backcountry, fatal accidents and injuries resulting from hypothermia-induced poor judgment and incoordination are all too common.

HOW WE LOSE AND CONSERVE HEAT

- *Radiation:* This is the direct loss of heat from a warm body to a cooler environment. Your head and neck account for more than 50 percent of your body's heat loss. Protective clothing, including a hat and scarf or neck gaiter, will help prevent this heat loss.

- *Conduction:* This is heat loss through direct physical contact between the body and a cooler surface. Insulating someone from the ground will help prevent this type of heat loss.

- *Convection:* This is heat loss by air movement circulating around the body and depends on the velocity of wind (wind chill factor). Windproof clothing and shelter will help reduce this type of heat loss. In a survival situation, wrapping a garbage bag around yourself or even using your pack as a bivy sac can help protect you from wind chill.

- *Evaporation:* When sweat or water evaporates or dries on your skin, it cools you. This type of heat loss can be minimized by using a vapor barrier liner under your clothing. Less recognized is the cooling effect of evaporation when you breathe. This can be reduced by breathing through a scarf or face mask.

YOUR THERMOSTAT IS IN YOUR SKIN!

Your perception of whether you are cold or warm depends more on your skin temperature than on your core temperature. Even when your core temperature is above normal, if your skin is cold you will feel cold and begin shivering (an involuntary condition in which your muscles twitch rapidly to generate additional body heat). Conversely, if your core temperature is low but your skin is warm, you feel warm, and do not shiver despite being hypothermic.

This underappreciated concept is important to understand if you spend time in the wilderness. If you warm a hypothermic individual's skin without providing any heat to the core (putting a chemical heat pad on the skin for example), you can extinguish the drive to shiver and cause the blood vessels on the skin to dilate, which will make him more hypothermic.

It is known that profoundly hypothermic victims sometimes rip off their clothes prior to death. This phenomenon, known as "paradoxical undressing," occurs because the constricted blood vessels near the body's surface suddenly dilate when the core temperature reaches a certain level and produce a sensation of warmth at the skin.

HOW TO RECOGNIZE AND TREAT HYPOTHERMIA

Hypothermia is often divided into mild and profound cases, based on a victim's temperature and behavior. The distinction is important, because the treatment and the worry factor are different. It can be hard to tell where one level starts and the other stops without a special low-reading thermometer. Certain signs and symptoms can often be used to gauge a victim's level of hypothermia.

MILD HYPOTHERMIA

At 95 degrees, a victim enters the zone of mild hypothermia.

Signs and Symptoms

1) The victim feels cold and shivering reaches its maximum level.
2) The victim maintains a normal level of consciousness, is alert, and has normal or only slightly impaired coordination.
3) At 93 degrees, the victim develops apathy, amnesia, slurred speech, and poor judgment.

Treatment

1) Get the victim into shelter and insulate him from the cold.
2) Replace any wet clothing with dry, insulated garments.
3) Give the victim warm food and lots of sugar containing fluids to drink. Elevating the core temperature of an average-sized individual one degree requires consuming about 60 kilocalories worth of a hot beverage. Because a quart of hot soup at 140 degrees provides about 30 kilocalories, a victim would have to consume two quarts to raise his temperature one degree. The sugar content

of the fluid, however, will provide added fuel for the victim's furnace so that he can generate his own internal heat.
4) Heat loss may be slowed by wrapping the victim in plastic bags or tarps as well as sleeping bags. Huddling together will reduce heat loss.
5) Resist the urge to use hot water bottles or heat packs; they can turn off the shivering mechanism and, by themselves, add very little heat to the core. Instead, bring water to a boil and have the victim inhale the steam, or build a fire.

PROFOUND HYPOTHERMIA
At 90 degrees, a victim is profoundly hypothermic.

Signs and Symptoms
1) The victim becomes weak and lethargic and has an altered mental state (disorientation, confusion, combative or irrational behavior, or coma).
2) The victim is uncoordinated (unable to walk a straight line, heel to toe, without stumbling).
3) At 88 degrees, the victim will stop shivering.
4) At 86 degrees, the victim's heart pumps less than two-thirds the normal amount of blood. Pulse and respirations will be half of normal.
5) At 83 degrees, the heart is very irritable and unstable and prone to developing irregularities, such as ventricular fibrillation. The victim is in danger of sudden cardiac arrest. Rough handling of the victim increases the potential for this to happen.

Treatment
First-aid treatment is aimed at preventing further cooling and stabilizing the victim.
1) Handle the victim gently. Rough handling may cause the victim's heart to fail.
2) Place the victim in a sleeping bag, or place blankets or clothing underneath and on top of him. Any heat that you can provide will probably not rewarm the victim, but will help prevent further cooling.

HYPOTHERMIA TABLE
*Temperature-Related Findings**

Core Temperature (degrees F)	Characteristics
99	Normal rectal temperature
98.6	Normal oral temperature
95	Maximum shivering
93	Poor judgment; slower movements
91.5	Clumsy movements; apathy
88	Shivering stops; stupor; altered level of consciousness
83-86	Heart is irritable and prone to arrhythmias
80	Voluntary motion ceases; pupils not reactive to light
72-77	Maximum risk of cardiac arrest

*General guidelines only; marked variations may occur.

3) A victim with a significantly altered mental state should not be allowed to eat or drink because of the potential for choking and vomiting.

4) Rewarming is best done in a hospital, because of the potential complications associated with profound hypothermia. Professional assistance is usually needed to evacuate a profoundly hypothermic victim.

CAUTION: First-aid management of hypothermic victims should not be based solely on measurements of body temperature, because obtaining an accurate temperature in the field can be difficult. It is only one consideration along with other observations and signs (such as an altered mental state) in guiding the decisions about appropriate treatment.

It may be difficult to distinguish between someone who is profoundly hypothermic and someone who is dead. The profoundly hypothermic person may have a pulse and respirations that are barely detectable. Double-check carefully, feeling for the carotid pulse for al least one full minute in a hypothermic victim, because the heart rate may be very slow. Place a cold glass surface next to the victim's mouth to see if it fogs up.

WHEN TO PERFORM CPR

If the victim is breathing or has any pulse, no matter how slow, do not initiate CPR. If there is no sign of a pulse or breathing after one minute, what to do next depends on your situation.

1) If you're alone or with only one other person, cover the victim and place him in a protected shelter. Place insulation on top and underneath him. Both individuals should go for help and stay together for safety.

2) If there are multiple rescuers, and it is safe to stay with the victim, begin CPR, while at least two people go for help. Chest compressions should be done at one-half the normal rate for a profoundly hypothermic individual.

Never assume that a profoundly hypothermic victim is dead until his body has been warmed and there are still no signs of life. Rarely, a victim who is without detectable signs of life, and presumed to be dead, will recover when rewarmed.

HEAT ILLNESS

Heat emergencies encompass a spectrum of illnesses, ranging from such minor reactions as muscle cramps to heat stroke, a life-threatening emergency.

There are some days when it is better to stay in the shade or camp indoors next to an air conditioner. The potential for developing heat illness is greatest in an environment that is both hot and humid. When the outside temperature exceeds 95 degrees F., evaporation of sweat from the body's surface is the only mechanism left to dissipate heat. If the humidity level then exceeds 80 percent, the ability to lose heat (from evaporation) declines dramatically, and the risk of developing heat illness soars. Sweat that merely drips from the skin and is not evaporated only contributes to dehydration without providing any cooling benefit.

Prevention
• Keep yourself hydrated

Dehydration is the most important contributing factor leading to heat illness. When you're overheated, the blood vessels near the skin dilate so that more blood can reach the surface and dissipate heat. If you're dehydrated, the blood vessels in the skin will constrict, and you will not be able to cool off as readily. More importantly, dehydration limits the ability of the body to sweat and evaporate heat.

Unfortunately, the body's dehydration sensor is not very sensitive. It waits until we're already two to five percent dehydrated before sounding the thirst alarm, and then shuts off prematurely, after we have replaced only two-thirds of the fluid defect. The best way to tell if you're hydrated is the urine-color gauge: clear to pale-yellow urine indicates that you're drinking enough fluids. Dark, yellow-colored urine indicates dehydration. (Note: some vitamins and medications can also turn urine a yellow/orange color.)

During exercise, you can easily sweat away one to two liters of water per hour. Trying to keep yourself hydrated requires a continual, conscious effort. Carry your water bottle where it is easily accessible and drink at least a pint every 20 minutes during a hike. As a general rule of thumb, in a hot environment, a person should drink one gallon of water for every 20 miles walked at night and two gallons for every 20 miles walked during the day.

The colder and tastier the beverage is, the more likely you will want to drink. Colder fluids are more easily absorbed from the stomach. Wrap the bottle in an article of clothing to help keep it cool, and add a powdered sports drink mix after disinfecting the water. Your body can absorb a carbohydrate containing beverage up to 30 percent faster than plain water. Diluted Gatorade (one-third to half strength) is ideal. Higher carbohydrate concentrations should be avoided because they can produce stomach cramps and delay absorption.

Salt lost in sweating can usually be replaced by a normal diet or by adding a small amount of salt to your drinking water. The ideal concentration is a 0.1% salt solution, which can be prepared by dissolving two 10-grain salt tablets or

1/4 teaspoon of table salt in a quart or water. The salt tablets should be crushed before attempting to dissolve them. Salt tablets should not be eaten by themselves. They irritate the stomach, produce vomiting, and do not treat the dehydration that is also present.

- **Hike in the early morning and late afternoon** when the sun is low and the heat less intense.
- **Avoid certain medications and drugs**
  1) Antihistamines found in many cold and allergy preparations decrease the rate of sweating.
  2) Antihypertension drugs such as beta-blockers, ace inhibitors, and diuretics can predispose you to heat illness.
  3) Amphetamines, PCP, and cocaine can all cause heat illness by increasing metabolic heat production.
- **Allow yourself adequate time to acclimatize before exercising for prolonged periods in the heat.**
  It takes about 10 days to become acclimatized to a hot environment. During that time, you will need to do about two hours of exercise each day. With acclimatization, your body becomes more efficient at cooling itself and you are less likely to suffer heat illness.
- **Wear clothing that is lightweight and loose-fitting for ventilation, and light-colored to reflect heat.**
- **Get plenty of rest:** A U.S. Army study found a correlation between lack of sleep, fatigue, and heat illness.

MINOR HEAT ILLNESS SYNDROMES

HEAT EDEMA
Swelling of the hands, feet, and ankles is common during the first few days in a hot environment. It is usually self-limited and does not require any treatment.

PRICKLY HEAT
This is a heat rash caused by plugged sweat glands in the skin. An itchy, red, bumpy rash develops on areas of the skin kept wet from sweating.

Treatment
1. Cool and dry the involved skin and avoid conditions that may induce sweating for awhile.
2. Antihistamines such as diphenhydramine (Benadryl®) may relieve itching.

HEAT CRAMPS
These are painful muscle spasms or cramps that usually occur in heavily exercised muscles. Spasms often begin after exertion has ended and a person is resting.

Treatment
Prevention and treatment consist of drinking plenty of fluids containing small amounts of salt (see above). Salt tablets taken alone are not advised. Rest in a cool environment and apply gentle, steady pressure to the cramped muscle.

HEAT SYNCOPE
When a person stands for a long time without moving, blood pools in the legs instead of returning to the heart. Standing in a hot environment also causes blood vessels on the surface of the skin to dilate, taking more blood away from the heart, which means there is less blood traveling to the brain. The combined effect can cause someone to faint from insufficient blood flow to the brain.

Treatment
Lying in a horizontal position with the legs elevated (Trendelenburg position) and cooling the skin will treat this condition.

HEAT EXHAUSTION
Heat exhaustion is the most common form of heat illness.

Signs and Symptoms
1) Malaise, headache, weakness, nausea, and loss of appetite.
2) Vomiting is common.
3) Dizziness when standing up from a sitting or lying position.

4) Dehydration.
5) Core temperature ranging from normal to moderately elevated (to 104 F).
6) Victims are sweating and have a normal mental state and remain coordinated.

Treatment
1) Stop all exertion and move the victim to a cool and shaded environment.
2) Remove restrictive clothing.
3) Administer oral rehydration solutions with plenty of water.
4) Ice or cold packs should be placed alongside the neck, chest wall, under the armpits, and in the groin. Fanning while splashing the skin with tepid water, or soaking the victim in cool water, are other cooling methods.

WARNING: Do not place ice directly against the skin for prolonged periods.

HEAT STROKE

The difference between heat stroke and heat exhaustion is that victims with heat stroke have abnormal mental states and neurological functions. They can be confused or display erratic or bizarre behavior, be disoriented, or seem off balance (the victim may appear intoxicated and be unable to walk a straight line). Seizures and coma are late manifestations. Sweating may still be present in heat stroke. Dry, hot skin is a very late finding and may not occur in some victims. Therefore, those who have a temperature above 105 F and an altered mental state should be considered to have heat stroke whether or not they are still sweating.

WHEN TO WORRY

Heat Stroke
Heat exhaustion that is not treated can progress to full-blown heat stroke, which has a mortality rate of 80 percent when not promptly treated. This is a life-threatening medical emergency.

Signs of Heat Stroke:
1) Elevated temperature (usually above 105 to 106 F.).
2) Altered mental state (confusion, disorientation, bizarre behavior, seizures, coma).
3) Rapid heart rate.
4) Low blood pressure.
5) Rapid respiration.
6) Sweating present or absent.

Treatment
1) Cool the victim as quickly as possible. Place ice or cold packs alongside the neck, chest wall, under the armpits, and in the groin. Wet the victim's skin with tepid water, and fan him rapidly to facilitate evaporative cooling. Immerse the victim in cool water if available.
2) Do not give the victim anything to drink because of the risk of vomiting and aspiration.
3) Acetaminophen and aspirin are not helpful in heat stroke and should not be given.
4) Treat for shock (See page 22).
5) Evacuate the victim immediately to the closest medical facility. Continue to cool along the way until the victim's temperature falls to 100 F to 101 F.
6) Recheck the temperature at least every 30 minutes.

DIVING MEDICINE

NEAR DROWNING

Treatment:

1) If a drowning victim is not breathing, mouth-to-mouth rescue breathing is the only first-aid treatment that matters (See page 12). Do not perform a Heimlich maneuver unless you are unable to breathe air into the victim because of an obstructed airway. A Heimlich maneuver will not drain water from the lungs, and may produce vomiting and aspiration.

2) Expect the victim to vomit during rescue breathing. When he does, log-roll him onto his side and sweep out the vomitus from his mouth. Then roll him back over and continue the resuscitation.

3) Evidence of trauma should be noted and spine immobilization undertaken if indicated by the mechanism of the event (See page 63).

4) Check for a pulse and begin chest compressions if necessary.

5) Remove the victim's wet clothing and cover him with blankets or other dry, warm material to prevent hypothermia. Be sure to protect the victim from conductive heat loss by also placing material between him and the ground or other cold surface.

6) All victims of a near drowning should be taken to a hospital for evaluation, even if they appear fully recovered. Delayed worsening of lung functioning may occur.

Following drowning in cold water (less than 50 degrees F), several victims have been revived even after 20 minutes of submersion (and two have survived more than one hour). These remarkable saves are presumably due to the protective effects of profound hypothermia. If possible, perform CPR on cold water drowning victims until they reach the hospital or until help arrives.

AIR EMBOLISM

An air embolism follows a rupture in the lungs between the air space and the blood vessels that carry blood back to the heart. When an air embolism occurs, bubbles of air are released into the arterial bloodstream. This can lead to a stroke, heart attack, headache, and/or confusion. An embolism usually occurs when a diver ascends too rapidly without adequately exhaling. Symptoms and signs may include unconsciousness, confusion, seizures, or chest pain after surfacing. Any symptoms that appear in a previously normal diver more than 10 minutes after surfacing are probably not due to an air embolism. Anyone suspected of having an air embolism should be placed in a head-down position (with the body at a 15 to 30-degree tilt) on his left side. Assist with mouth-to-mouth breathing if necessary and immediately transport the victim to a medical facility. The treatment for air embolism is recompression in a hyperbaric chamber. When available, oxygen can be administered at the rate of 10 liters per minute by face mask.

DECOMPRESSION SICKNESS (BENDS)

When a diver descends in the water, nitrogen is present in the compressed air is absorbed by the body. If a diver ascends too rapidly, microscopic bubbles of nitrogen exit the blood stream into the surrounding tissue, causing "the bends." Symptoms can begin immediately after ascent or may develop over a period of hours. Symptoms include joint pain, numbness and tingling of the arms and legs, back pain, fatigue, weakness, inability to control the bladder or bowel, paralysis, headache, confusion, dizziness, nausea, vomiting, difficulty in speaking, itching, skin mottling, shortness of breath, cough, and collapse. Anyone suspected of having the bends should be treated with immediate oxygen therapy (10 liters per minute by face mask). Transport the victim to the nearest medical facility. Treatment for the bends is recompression in a hyperbaric chamber. Divers should not fly for 12 hours after a no-decompression dive and for 24 hours following a decompression dive.

NITROGEN NARCOSIS

At depths of greater than 90 feet, divers are at risk for this disorder, caused by the absorption of nitrogen into the bloodstream. Symptoms include confusion, euphoria, bad judgment and unconsciousness. Never dive alone. A diving partner exhibiting any of the above symptoms should be assisted slowly to the surface.

EAR SQUEEZE

If a diver cannot equalize the pressure on the eardrum by forcing air through the Eustachian tube and into the middle ear, the eardrum stretches inward and may rupture. A rupture allows water to enter the middle ear, resulting in pain, dizziness, nausea, vomiting, and disorientation. If this happens, a diver should remain calm and slowly ascend to the surface. Allow the ear to dry on its own. Do not insert anything into the ear, as it may increase the damage to the eardrum. Obtain immediate medical assistance.

SINUS SQUEEZE

If air cannot be forced into the sinuses during descent, the sinuses contract, causing pain and bleeding. If a sinus squeeze occurs, slowly ascend to the surface. The victim may go on to develop sinusitis and should be placed on antibiotics (ampicillin, erythromycin, or penicillin) for eight days. Treat the congestion with nasal or oral decongestants.

A "reverse squeeze" occurs during ascent, when air expands in the sinus. This can be very painful, but will resolve itself.

HAZARDOUS MARINE LIFE

Many types of marine life can be hazardous to unwary victims. People spending time near the ocean should be aware of the potential dangers presented by the marine life residing there. One of the best ways to avoid problems associated with hazardous marine life is to become familiar with the creatures which cause problems and learn how to avoid them.

SHARKS

Shark bites can cause severe damage or death, usually through blood loss and shock. See wound management (see page 86). Even small shark bites should be examined by a physician. Any animal bite is at high risk for infection and should not be sewn or taped tightly shut. Allow the wound to drain and begin antibiotic therapy (doxycycline or trimethoprim with sulfamethoxazole).

Sharks also have very rough skin and can impart a nasty scrape. Treat the victim as you would for a second-degree burn.

BARRACUDA AND MORAY EELS
Both these types of bites should be treated as you would a shark bite.

CORAL AND BARNACLES
To avoid infection from coral and barnacle cuts and scrapes, scrub the area vigorously with soap and water, then flush the wound with a large amount of water. Continue by flushing with a one-half strength solution of hydrogen peroxide and water. Rinse the area again with clean water. Apply antibiotic ointment and cover with a nonadherent dressing. The wound should be cleaned twice a day. If the wound shows any sign of infection (increased redness, pus, swollen lymph glands, or red streaks near the wound), consult a physician. Antibiotic therapy includes trimethoprim with sulfamethoxazole, ciprofloxacin or tetracycline.

SWIMMERS ITCH, SEAWEED DERMATITIS AND SEA BATHERS ERUPTION
While these conditions are caused by different entities, the treatment is the same. Skin reactions, including red, itchy areas, often with blisters and/or weeping, develop after swimming. This can be treated by washing with soap and water, followed by a rinse of isopropyl (rubbing) alcohol 40 to 70 percent. Apply hydrocortisone cream 1 percent two times a day. If the reaction is severe or persists, see a doctor.

FISH HANDLERS' DISEASE
This is an infection that usually starts in small nicks or cuts on fish handlers' hands. It is characterized by a skin rash erupting two to seven days after exposure. Usually the skin surrounding the cut will appear red or violet-colored and will be slightly warm and tender. Treatment includes antibiotic therapy (penicillin, cephalexin, or erythromycin).

SPONGES
Contact with sponges can lead to a poison ivy-type reaction characterized by redness, itching and swelling. Treat by soaking the affected area with vinegar (5 percent acetic

acid) for 10 to 15 minutes. Dry the skin and repeatedly apply and remove sticky adhesive tape to the area to remove any embedded sponge spicules. Repeat the vinegar soak for five minutes or apply rubbing alcohol for one minute. Apply hydrocortisone cream 1 percent two times a day until the irritation is resolved.

JELLYFISH

These animals inflict painful (occasionally life-threatening) stings. Stings occur when the skin comes into contact with the tentacles, which contain millions of venomous stinging cells. Broken off pieces of jellyfish that wash up on the beach can remain toxic for months and should not be handled. The venom from the box jellyfish (from northern Australia) can kill in minutes by causing abnormal heart rhythms and cardio-pulmonary collapse. The symptoms and treatment for jellyfish stings are to some degree similar for the Portuguese man-of-war (bluebottle), box jellyfish (sea wasp), Irukandji, fire coral, stinging hydroid, sea nettle, and sea anemone.

Symptoms range from mild burning and redness to severe pain and blistering. Victims may also experience nausea, vomiting, shortness of breath, and low blood pressure.

Treatment of Jellyfish Stings:
1) Immediately apply vinegar (acetic acid 5 percent). If vinegar is not available, flush the area with sea water. Cold packs or ice may relieve pain following a man-of-war sting. Do not rinse with fresh water or apply ice directly to the skin.
2) Apply vinegar (5 percent acetic acid) or rubbing alcohol (40 to 70 percent) for 30 minutes or until the pain subsides. If these products are not available, use household ammonia (one fourth strength). Urine and meat tenderizer also have limited usefulness.
3) Remove any embedded particles using a Splinter Picker or tweezers. Be careful not to touch the fragments with your bare hands.
4) Apply shaving cream or a baking soda paste. Shave the area using a razor or other sharp-edged object.
5) Reapply the vinegar or alcohol soak for 15 minutes.

6) Apply a layer of hydrocortisone cream 1 percent two times a day.
7) Seek medical attention if a large area is affected, if the victim is very old or very young, or if there are significant signs of illness (nausea, vomiting, weakness, shortness of breath, chest pain, etc.).
8) If the victim was stung on the mouth or has any respiratory tract involvement, do not give him anything by mouth. Monitor his condition constantly to ensure an unobstructed airway and transport him to definitive medical care.
9) If the sting is from the Australian box jellyfish, seek immediate assistance in addition to completing the above steps. An antivenin is available.

SEA URCHINS

Sea urchin spines are venomous. The puncture wounds from these animals can cause difficulty in breathing, weakness, or collapse. To treat this injury, immerse the affected area in hot water to tolerance (110 to 113 F./43.3 to 45 C.). Carefully remove only visible spines. Do not attempt to clean the wound thoroughly. Consult a physician. If the victim shows any signs of infection, administer trimethoprim-sulfamethoxazole, ciprofloxacin, or tetracycline.

SEA CUCUMBERS

Treat any skin irritation resulting from contact with a sea cucumber the same as a jellyfish sting. If the eyes are involved, flush with at least a quart of water. Seek immediate medical attention.

STINGRAYS

Injury from a stingray includes both deep puncture wounds or lacerations and envenomation. Symptoms include pain, bleeding, weakness, vomiting, headache, fainting, shortness of breath, paralysis, collapse, and on occasion, death. Rinse the wound with water (fresh or sea water). Immerse the area in hot water to tolerance (110 to 113 F/43.3 to 45 C) for 30 to 90 minutes. Scrub the wound well with soap and water. Do not attempt to close the wound: A serious infection could result. If a physician is more than 12 hours away, administer an antibiotic (trimethoprim with sulfamethoxazole, cipro-floxacin, or tetracycline.

CATFISH

Treat as you would a stingray wound. Hot water can provide significant pain relief.

SCORPIONFISH

Treat the same as a stingray wound. Seek immediate medical attention if the victim appears intoxicated (weak, vomiting, short of breath, or unconscious). In Australia, an antivenin is available.

SEA SNAKES

Sea snakes bite with four fangs. The venom can cause paralysis, destruction of red blood cells, and generalized muscle damage. The site of the bite may not be very painful. If symptoms do not develop within six to eight hours of a bite, venom is not present to any great degree in the wound. Symptoms include weakness, paralysis, lockjaw, drooping eyelids, difficulty speaking, vomiting, darkened urine and difficulty breathing. Treat this emergency as you would a land snake bite (See page 129).

SEAFOOD POISONING

SCROMBOID POISONING

Scromboid poisoning results from eating contaminated fish (usually tuna, mackerel, bonito, skipjack, mahi-mahi, anchovies, sardines, or Australian ocean salmon). The fish may or may not have a peppery or metallic taste. Almost immediately after eating the fish, the victim will develop symptoms similar to an allergic reaction. These symptoms may include becoming flushed, itching, hives, abdominal pain, nausea, diarrhea, and a low-grade fever. Treat this reaction with Benadryl® (diphenhydramine) every six to eight hours until it resolves.

PARALYTIC SHELLFISH POISONING

Paralytic shellfish poisoning is caused by eating contaminated shellfish. These animals are usually quarantined each year while they feed on poisonous microorganisms. Minutes after eating the shellfish, the victim may experience numbness of the mouth, becoming lightheaded and weak. Symptoms also include drooling, difficulty swallowing, incoordination, headache, thirst, diarrhea, abdominal pain, blurred vision, sweating and rapid heartbeat. Seek immediate medical attention.

FISHHOOK INJURIES

Fishhooks have a barb just behind the tip and are curved so that the more force applied to the hook, the deeper it penetrates. The barb does not allow the hook to be backed out. The classic method of advancing the barb through the skin and cutting the hook so that the remaining shank can be backed out is effective, but there is an easier and less painful technique.

Removing a Fishhook

Pass a length of string, fishing line, suture material or dental floss through and around the bend of the hook. Grasp the ends of the string and, while applying gentle downward pressure on the shank to disengage the barb, yank on the string **(Fig. 61)**.

After removing the hook, clean the entry point with an antiseptic towelette or soap and water.

CAUTION: Fishhooks embedded in the eye should be left in place and secured with tape, the eye covered with a metal patch or cup, and the victim transported to an ophthalmologist for definitive care.

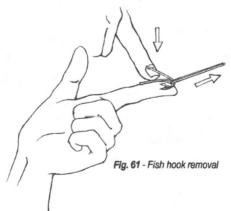

Fig. 61 - Fish hook removal

LIGHTNING

Lightning kills more people every year in the United States than all other natural disasters combined. Carrying or wearing metal objects, such as an ice axe, umbrella, backpack frame, or even a hairpin, increases the chances of being hit.

To calculate the approximate distance in miles from a flash of lightning, count in seconds from the time you see the flash to when you hear the thunder, then divide by five.

Prevention
- When a thunderstorm threatens, seek shelter in a building or inside a vehicle (not a convertible).
- Occupants of tents should stay as far away from the poles and wet cloths as possible.
- Do not stand underneath a tall tree in an open area or on a hill top.
- Get out and away from open water.
- Get away from tractors and other metal farm equipment.
- Get off bicycles and golf carts.
- Stay away from wire fences, clotheslines, metal pipes, and other metallic paths which could carry lightning to you from some distance.
- Avoid standing in small, isolated sheds or other small structures in open areas.
- In a forest, seek shelter in a low area under a thick growth of saplings or small trees. In an open area, go to a low place such as a ravine or valley.
- If you are totally in the open, stay far away from single trees to avoid lightning splashes. Drop to your knees and bend forward, putting your hands on your knees. If available, place insulating material (e.g. sleeping pad, life jacket, rope) between you and the ground. Do not lie flat on the ground.

LIGHTNING CAN CAUSE INJURY BY FOUR MECHANISMS:

1. DIRECT HIT
Lightning directly strikes a person in the open. It usually does not enter the body, but instead is conducted over the

skin surface ("flashover"), producing a variety of injuries. The greatest damage may occur to skin beneath metal objects worn by the victim, such as jewelry, belt buckles, or zippers, which tend to disrupt the flashover and allow current to penetrate. Current may also penetrate the body through the eyes, ears, and mouth, causing deeper injuries to those parts. The victim is exposed to a tremendous electromagnetic field, which can disrupt the workings of the brain, lungs and heart and lead to a cardiac and respiratory arrest. Finally, the instant vaporization of any moisture on the victim's skin can blast apart his clothing and shoes.

2. SPLASH
A more common scenario is for the victim to be struck by lightning "splash," which occurs when a bolt first hits an object, such as a tree or another person, and then "jumps" to the victim who may have found shelter nearby. Splashes may also occur from person to person who are standing close together.

3. STEP VOLTAGE
Lightning hits the ground or a nearby object and the current spreads like a wave in a pond to the victims. Step voltage is often to blame when several people are hurt by a single lightning bolt.

4. BLUNT TRAUMA
The explosive force of the pressure waves created by lightning can cause blunt trauma, such as spleen or liver injuries and ruptured ear drums.

TYPES OF INJURIES

1. HEART AND LUNG
Lightning can cause a cardiac arrest and paralyze the lungs. The heart will often restart on its own, but because the lungs are still not working, the heart will stop again from lack of oxygen.

2. NEUROLOGIC INJURIES
The victim may be knocked unconscious and suffer temporary paralysis, especially in the legs. Seizures, confusion, blindness, deafness, and inability to remember what happened may result.

3. TRAUMATIC INJURIES
Bruises, fractures, dislocations, spinal injury, chest and abdominal injuries from the shock wave may occur. Ruptured eardrums can result in hearing loss.

4. BURNS
Superficial first or second-degree burns are more common than severe burns after a lightning strike and form distinctive fern patterns on the skin.

Treatment
Lightning strike victims are not "charged" and thus pose no hazard to rescuers.

1. The immediate treatment of lightning strike victims differs from other situations in which you have multiple trauma victims. Rather than adhere to the standard rescue dogma of ignoring the victims who appear dead and giving priority to those who are still alive, after a lightning strike, treat those victims first who appear dead, because they may ultimately recover if quickly given mouth-to-mouth rescue breathing and CPR. If you're successful in obtaining a pulse with CPR, continue rescue breathing until the victim begins to breathe on his own or you are no longer able to continue the resuscitation.
2. Stabilize and splint any fractures.
3. Initiate and maintain spinal precautions if indicated.

PREPARING FOR FOREIGN TRAVEL

Nearly one-half of travelers to developing countries become ill during their visit. Diseases such as polio, malaria, and typhoid fever that are uncommon in the U.S. are a threat to travelers who visit areas where poor sanitation and contaminated food and water exist. International travelers should contact their local health department, physician or travel medicine clinic at least six weeks prior to departure, to obtain current health information on countries they plan to visit and to begin receiving vaccinations. Beside vaccinations, travelers should undergo medical and dental physical exams prior to departure, and obtain medications that you may need during travel from a physician (See Appendix B).

The WHO maintains recommendations regarding vaccine requirements for international travelers, with its annual publication of vaccination requirements and health advice in International travel and Health (with electronic access through its website at www.who.int/ith). Updates on official changes in vaccine requirements for travel are summarized in the Summary of Health Information for International Travel, published biweekly by the Division of Quarantine at the CDC (www.cdc.gov/travel/blusheet.htm). The CDC also develops guidelines and information for international travelers, which are contained in its publication, Health Information for International Travel (published on a biannual basis, with electronic access through the CDC website at www.cdc.gov/travel). Similar information and guidelines are also published for use in Canada

This can be accessed at http://www.hc-sc.gc.ca/pphb-dg-spsp/publicat/cig-gci/.

You may also call the Centers for Disease Control and Prevention automated travelers' hotline from a touch-tone phone 24 hours a day at (404)332-4559. This service provides up-to-date information on requirements and recommendations for international travel.

TIMING OF VACCINES

Vaccinations should begin at least six weeks prior to departure. Travelers often request vaccinations at the last minute, leading to concerns about the appropriate timing and spacing of injections. In general, inactivated vaccines or toxoids, such as those for hepatitis B, cholera, typhoid, rabies, plague, influenza, tetanus, diphtheria, or inactivated polio, may be given simultaneously at separate sites.

Live vaccines, such as those for measles, mumps, rubella, and oral polio, can be administered simultaneously with an inactivated vaccine, except those for cholera and yellow fever. Immune globulin given for Hepatitis A can be given simultaneously with inactivated vaccines and toxoids. Live vaccines should be given at least two weeks before immune globulin or three to five months afterwards.

REQUIRED VACCINE

YELLOW FEVER

Yellow fever is an acute viral hemorrhagic disease transmitted to humans by mosquitoes in tropical Africa and South America. Yellow fever (YF) transmission occurs in jungle and urban cycles in South America, with peak transmission during the months of January through March.

Countries located in YF endemic areas such as African countries (Burkina Faso, Cameroon, Congo, Cote D'Ivoire, Democratic Republic of Congo, Gabon, Ghana, Liberia, Mali, Mauritania, Niger, Rwanda, Sao Tome, Togo) and one in South America (French Guiana) require proof of yellow fever vaccination from all arriving travelers.

The vaccine is a live attenuated virus. The immunization must be given no less than 10 days prior to planned date of entry. Vaccine administration is documented and stamped on the appropriate page of the International Certificate of Vaccination. This proof of vaccination is sometimes required during crossing of international borders, particularly in Africa, or if flying from an infected country to a non-infected country, even if the stay in the endemic country was a brief transit stop.

Yellow fever vaccine is approved for use in all persons

over nine months of age who have no YF vaccine contraindication.

The primary schedule for yellow fever vaccine in adults is a single 0.5 ml injection given subcutaneously. The duration of immunity from one dose of the vaccine is estimated to last for 10 years or longer. A booster dose is recommended for persons with continued risk of exposure 10 years from the last dose.

Yellow fever vaccine can be administered concurrently or at any time before or after immune globulin products given for hepatitis A prophylaxis.

RECOMMENDED VACCINES

DIPHTHERIA, MEASLES, MUMPS, RUBELLA, AND POLIO are childhood immunizations that all international travelers should keep up to date. Tetanus should be updated with a booster every 10 years. Travelers born after 1956, who have not received two doses of measles vaccine or do not have a well-documented history of having the illness as a child, should receive a single injection of the measles vaccine. Travelers who have previously completed a primary polio series and have never had a booster should receive a booster dose of oral polio vaccine (OPV). Further information on this can be found on the World Health Organization website: www.who.int/vaccines/GlobalSummary/Immunization/CountryProfileSelect.cfm. Cases of measles and varicella have been reported as travel-acquired infections among international travelers, and these common childhood infectious diseases are known to cause more serious disease in infections acquired by adults.

CHOLERA VACCINE

The highest incidence of cholera cases in the world is being reported from Africa (predominantly from South Africa and Democratic Republic of Congo, Mozambique, and Malawi).

Cholera vaccine is not required for entry into any country under current WHO International Health Regulations. Cholera vaccine is not recommended for the short-term tourists traveling to an endemic country. Immunization may be recommended for travelers who plan extensive travel or work in highly endemic/epidemic areas under unsanitary conditions and without access to Western style medical care.

The newer cholera vaccines are the live attenuated oral vaccines and killed whole cell (KWC) oral vaccines.

The live attenuated oral cholera CVD-103 HgR vaccine is extremely safe. The vaccine should not be given to immunosuppressed people or those with chronic liver disease. There is no data on safety in pregnant women. The killed whole cell oral cholera vaccine also appears to be extremely safe; the only contraindication is intolerance to a previously administered dose.

The KWC vaccine is taken in two doses separated by seven to 42 days. A booster is recommended every two years for repeated exposure.

HEPATITIS A VACCINE

Hepatitis A is a viral infection transmitted by contaminated food or water or even by direct person-to-person contact. The risk of Hepatitis A infection is highest in developing countries with poor sanitation and food hygiene.

Hepatitis A vaccine (Havrix®) is recommended for travelers going to developing or third-world countries where sanitation may be poor. The vaccine is given as a single injection to adults and as two injections one month apart to children less than 17 years of age. A booster injection six to 12 months later is also recommended. It takes at least three weeks to be protected after the initial injection. Travelers who will arrive in a high-risk area less than three works from the date of their vaccination should also receive hepatitis immune globulin. A single injection of immune globulin is good for up to five months, depending on the dose. Studies have shown that immune globulin prepared in the U.S. carries no risk of transmission of AIDS. It is also safe to use in pregnancy.

HEPATITIS B VACCINE

Although hepatitis B (HB) vaccine was incorporated into the schedule of routine childhood immunizations starting in the late 1980s, HB vaccine is a recommended travel vaccine for certain susceptible adult travelers who are going to areas where the disease is endemic.

INDICATIONS
Travelers who anticipate exposure to blood or body secretions (health care personnel, relief workers), unprotected sexual exposures with members of the local population or others, and adventure travelers who are at higher risk of accidents and needing medical attention.

DOSING SCHEDULES FOR ADULTS
For adults, the dose of the HB vaccine is 1.0 ml given intramuscularly in the deltoid muscle. The primary immunization schedule consists of three vaccine doses given on a schedule of zero, one, and six months. The vaccine should be given intramuscularly for best response, but hepatitis B vaccine should not be given in the buttock because this route of administration has been associated with a lower immune response.

ACCELERATED SCHEDULES
The three-dose primary series may be accelerated to be administered at zero, one, and four months or zero, two, and four months where the second dose should be given at least one month after the first dose and the third dose should be given at least four months after the first dose and at least two months after the second dose (zero, one, four months or zero, two, four months).

JAPANESE ENCEPHALITIS VACCINE
Japanese encephalitis (JE) is a mosquito-transmitted virus infection that is endemic in Asia and potentially fatal. In temperate regions the transmission season generally extends from April through November with a peak in July through September. In tropical or subtropical regions of Oceania and Southeast Asia, transmission may occur year-round.

INDICATIONS
Consider JEV for travelers who plan to spend two to four weeks or more in endemic areas, particularly in rural areas,

during the transmission season. Travelers planning extensive unprotected outdoor, evening and nighttime exposure in rural areas may be at risk even if the trip is very short. Risk of transmission is higher in rural areas, especially where pigs are raised and where rice fields, marshes and standing pools of water provide breeding grounds for mosquitoes and feed for birds.

DOSING SCHEDULES FOR ADULTS

The primary schedule in adults is a series of three doses of 1.0 ml of JEV administered by subcutaneous injection on a schedule of 0, 7, and 30 days. The immunity should last for at least three years after primary immunization series.

MENINGOCOCCAL VACCINE

Neisseria meningitidis spreads through the air via droplets of contaminated respiratory secretions, or through person-to-person contact (kissing, sharing cigarettes and drinking glasses, etc.).

INDICATIONS

Meningococcal vaccine is recommended for travelers to some countries of Africa during the dry season from December through June, especially if prolonged contact with the local populace is likely. The countries include Benin, Burkina Faso, Cameroon, Central African Republic, Chad, Cote D'Ivoire, Djibouti, Ethiopia, Gambia, Ghana, Guinea, Guinea Bissau, Mali, Niger, Nigeria, Senegal, Sudan, Somalia, and Togo.

DOSING SCHEDULES FOR ADULTS

The quadrivalent meningococcal polysaccharide vaccine consists of a single dose of 0.5 ml by subcutaneous injection to adults. This vaccine should be administered one to two weeks before departure.

ADVERSE EVENTS

Minor side-effects consisting of local pain, swelling and redness of the skin at the site of injection, and rarely, a low-grade fever, have been reported.

RABIES

Pre-exposure vaccination against rabies is recommended for travelers to endemic areas who are at increased risk, such as veterinarians, animal handlers, spelunkers and biologists. A series of three injections over three weeks is required.

TYPHOID

Typhoid fever is a infection transmitted by contaminated food and water. High risk areas for contracting this illness include Southern Asia; the Middle East; East, West and Central Africa; and Central and South America. Although an injectable vaccine is still available, the newer oral typhoid vaccine is preferable.

1) Typhoid injectable vaccine: This consists of two injections given at least four weeks apart. It is good for three years. It is about 70 percent effective in preventing the disease, and is usually associated with one or two days of post-injection side effects. These include discomfort at the site of injection, fever, headache and flu-like symptoms.
2) Oral typhoid vaccine: This consists of ingesting four capsules on alternate days for a total of four capsules over eight days. A booster is required every seven years. Adverse reactions are uncommon.

MALARIA

Malaria is an infection of the bloodstream by a parasite transmitted to humans through the bite of the Anopheles mosquito. After a period ranging from a week to months, a flu-like illness develops, characterized by recurrent fevers, chills, headache, weakness, and lethargy. Fever in a traveler who has returned from a malaria-endemic area should be attributed to malaria until proven otherwise. More than 300 million people are infected each year, with two to three million deaths; it is a significant health threat to travelers.

PREVENTION TECHNIQUES

The best way to prevent malaria is to avoid the mosquito. In Nepal, for example, there is almost no risk in the city of Katmandu. Traveling to more rural areas increases the risk. The Anopheles mosquito feeds at night. Thus, maximum precautions should be taken from dusk to dawn. It takes only one bite from an infected mosquito to acquire the disease. One should wear thin, loose clothing that covers the arms and legs. At dusk, tuck your pants into your socks or shoes, and tape the cuffs of your shirt sleeves closed. Screens, mosquito nets, and repellents should be used at night. The most effective repellents contain up to 35% DEET (N-N, diethyl-toluamide). The duration of action is between two and six hours, depending on the concentration of DEET, how much the wearer perspires and how hungry the mosquito is. There have been rare case reports of adverse reactions to DEET, ranging from skin rashes to central nervous system (brain) disorders. Spraying or soaking clothing and bed nets with Permethrin and letting them air dry before use is also very helpful.

DRUGS TO PREVENT MALARIA

No anti-malarial drug is absolutely effective. A traveler can still develop the disease regardless of how many medications they take. The number of effective drugs is rapidly shrinking, due to the ability of the parasite to develop resistance to antibiotics. By the time you have finished reading this booklet, the number of places where malaria is resistant to chloroquine (a common drug used for prevention) will have increased. Updated information can be obtained by referring to Health Information for International Travel (see appendix) or by calling the CDC Malaria Hotline by phone (404) 332-4555 or by fax (404) 332-4565.

CHLOROQUINE

There are only a few places left in the world where chloroquine is still effective in preventing malaria. Chloroquine is recommended for travel to Central America west of the Panama Canal Zone, Mexico, Haiti, the Dominican Republic, Egypt, and most countries in the Middle East (chloroquine resistance has been reported in Iran, Yemen and Oman). The drug is generally safe, but side effects can include nausea, diarrhea, and upset stomach. It is taken once weekly, beginning two weeks prior to departure, continued weekly during travel in malarious areas and for four weeks after leaving such areas.

MEFLOQUINE

Mefloquine is now the most widely prescribed drug for the prevention of malaria in parts of the world where the parasite is resistant to chloroquine. The adult dose is 250 mg once a week. The pediatric dose varies according to the weight of the child. Check with your pediatrician. Mefloquine should be started one to two weeks before travel and continued for four weeks after leaving the endemic area. Mefloquine should not be taken during pregnancy, or if on a beta-blocker or calcium channel blocker medication.

Mefloquine can occasionally produce serious adverse reactions such as acute psychoses, hallucinations, anxiety, and seizures. Other side effects include nausea, upset stomach and diarrhea.

DOXYCYCLINE

An alternative to mefloquine is doxycycline 100 mg daily. This drug is not advised for pregnant women or children under eight years of age. It can also cause a rash in users exposed to the sun.

PROGUANIL (PALUDRINE)

This drug may be used for malaria prevention where there is resistance to chloroquine. The adult dose is 200 mg daily along with weekly chloroquine.

MALARONE
Atavaquone in combination with proguanil is available as the drug Malarone and can be taken to prevent chloroquine-resistant malaria. The drug is taken at the same time each day with food or a milky drink. The drug should be started two days before entering a malaria-endemic area and continued for seven days after return. The adult dose is one tablet (250 ml atovaquone/100 mg proguanil) per day.

FANSIDAR
This is a combination drug containing pyrimethamine and sulfadoxine. Because of the drug's association with an unacceptably high incidence of toxic side effects when used for prevention, it is generally reserved only for treatment.

LATENT MALARIA
Certain forms of malaria (P. vivax) can hide in the liver and cause illness for as long as four years after returning from an endemic country. The drug Primaquine®, taken after the traveler has left a malaria area, can prevent this from occurring.

MEDICAL ADVICE & ASSISTANCE

There are organizations that can help travelers prepare medically for foreign excursions and provide assistance once they arrive.

The International Association for Medical Assistance to Travelers (IAMAT), established in 1960, is a voluntary organization of hospitals, health care centers, and physicians. It has more than 3,000 English-speaking, Western-trained doctors in over 140 countries. All fees are standardized. Each year, the IAMAT publishes an updated directory of its member physicians, as well as pamphlets on immunization requirements, climate charts, malaria and schistosomiasis risk information. IAMAT membership is free. Contact IAMAT at 417 Center St., Lewiston, NY 14092, (716) 754-4883 www.iamat.org.

COMMON TRAVEL DISEASES

TYPHOID FEVER
Symptoms usually begin 10 to 14 days after exposure to the bacteria.

Signs and Symptoms
Fever is usually the first sign of disease. Headache, fatigue, abdominal cramps, diarrhea or constipation, and dizziness often occur. A red rash that blanches with pressure sometimes develops on the trunk.

Treatment
Most victims get better on their own after three to four weeks. A few individuals will develop severe complications including intestinal perforation and peritonitis.

Antibiotics (ampicillin or Ciprofloxacin®) can be used to treat the illness.

DENGUE FEVER
Dengue is a very common mosquito-transmitted viral infection. It is now endemic in Asia, the South Pacific, the Caribbean Basin, Mexico, Central and South America, and Africa.

Signs and Symptoms
The illness is characterized by sudden onset of high fever, severe frontal headache, and joint and muscle pains, which can be so painful that it is sometimes called "breakbone fever." Many victims have nausea, vomiting and develop a rash three to five days after onset of fever. The symptoms can be similar to and even be mistaken for malaria.

Treatment
The illness is usually self-limited and lasts about a week. Occasionally, a victim will remain very weak for up to one month, or develop a severe and fatal syndrome called dengue hemorrhagic fever. There is no specific treatment and a vaccine is not available.

SCHISTOSOMIASIS

This is a parasitic disease transmitted by freshwater snails that excrete the parasite into the water. The parasite then penetrates the skin of humans during bathing or swimming in freshwater ponds, lakes, or rivers. The countries where schistosomiasis is most common include Brazil, Egypt and sub-Saharan Africa, southern China, the Philippines, and Southeast Asia.

Signs and Symptoms

Symptoms usually start two to three weeks after exposure and include fever, loss of appetite, abdominal pain, weakness, headaches, joint and muscle pain, diarrhea, nausea, cough, and itchy rash. Infection of the brain can produce seizures and visual loss.

Treatment

Praziquantel (Biltricide), an antiparasitic drug, will effectively cure the illness.

MALARIA (See page 173)

CUTANEOUS MYIASIS (Botfly infection)

Botfly (Dermatobia hominis) infections are common in travelers to the jungles of Central and South America. The female fly attaches her eggs to the body of another arthropod (usually a mosquito), which then transfers the egg to the skin of a human when it lands for a meal. The eggs hatch immediately and the larva crawls into the skin through the bite wound, where it continues to grow. Initially it looks and feels like another mosquito bite. The victim is eventually alerted that something else is going on when the bump gets larger over time and becomes quite painful. He may experience a sensation of movement within the bump. A characteristic central opening (breathing hole) drains clear fluid when the bump is squeezed. The developing larva just underneath the skin can be mistaken for a bacteria infected bite, leading to unnecessary antibiotics or worse, incision and drainage.

Treatment
First cover the opening with DEET-containing repellent or permethrine and wait about 30 minutes for it to kill the larva. When the larva dies, it releases its attachment to the skin. Then, forcefully squeeze the skin adjacent to the bump to extrude the larva.

'WEISS ADVICE'

[IMPROVISED TECHNIQUE]

Smoking-out Botfly Larva
Blowing cigarette smoke onto your hand will create a lethal deposit of tobacco which can then be transferred to the bump and smeared over the hole. Leave in place for 20 to 30 minutes before squeezing. Duct tape, smeared with petroleum jelly or nail polish remover will also suffocate the larva if placed tightly over the hole.

MOTION SICKNESS
Bumpy bus rides, air and ocean travel are often associated with motion sickness. It is caused by fluid movement in the inner ear. Symptoms include pale skin, sweating, nausea, and weakness. These symptoms are usually made worse by alcohol ingestion, emotional upset, noxious odors, and ear infections. Symptoms will not dissipate until the inner ear has had a chance to acclimate to motion (usually within a few days), or is treated with medication.

To control motion sickness, first try fixing your eyes on a steady point in the distance. Move to the center of the boat, plane or bus, where motion is minimized. If particularly prone to motion sickness, you can try taking meclizine (Antivert®) 25 mg orally or dimenhydranate (Dramamine®) 50 mg orally every six to 12 hours, beginning two to three hours before travel. Benadryl® has also been shown to help prevent and treat motion sickness. For the medication to be most effective, it should be started before encountering a situation that can lead to motion sickness.

JET LAG

Jet lag is common among travelers who cross several time zones. While the symptoms are usually mild, it can be difficult for a person to function until the body's rhythms have had a chance to adjust. Symptoms include irritability, insomnia, headache, loss of appetite, and a general feeling of malaise. Dehydration, which commonly occurs on long flights, may be a factor in the severity of jet lag. Drinking fluids and avoiding alcohol until adjusted to the new time zone can be very helpful. A low dose of a short-acting sleeping pill (Ambien® or Halcion®) can be taken for the first two to three days after arrival to facilitate sleep at night.

Exposure to bright light for five to seven hours a day for two to three days may help reset one's internal clock. Travelers going eastward should expose themselves to bright light in the early morning, while those traveling westward should expose themselves to bright light in the late afternoon.

The hormone melatonin (5 mg), taken at bedtime for two days before travel, then for three days after arrival, may also help reset the body's internal clock. Little, however, is known about the long-term safety of melatonin. It should not be taken by children, women who are pregnant, nursing or trying to conceive, or people with cancer, severe allergies or on steroid therapy.

'WEISS ADVICE'

[IMPROVISED TECHNIQUE]

Curbing Motion Sickness

Ginger root has been shown to very effective in curbing the nausea caused by motion sickness. Ginger is ordinarily taken in the form of capsules, each containing 500 mg of the powdered herb. The average recommended daily dose is between two to three grams. It may also be consumed as a tea or in the extract form. There are no reports of severe toxicity in humans from eating recommended amounts of ginger.

APPENDIX A

WATER DISINFECTION

There are three proven techniques for removing infectious organisms (bacteria, viruses, parasites) from water: filters, boiling and chemical treatment.

FILTERS

Filters are commercially available with pore sizes small enough to remove Giardia organisms and most bacteria from water. Many now also have iodine resins which can kill viruses.

BOILING

Much of the time required to bring water to a boil works toward disinfecting it. By the time it reaches boiling, the water is safe to drink. Although the boiling point of water decreases as you go higher in altitude, this should not make a difference, since almost all organisms are killed well below the boiling point of water.[1]

CHEMICALS

The two most common chemicals used to disinfect water are chlorine and iodine. Iodine is preferred over chlorine in the backcountry because it:

  1) is less affected by pH and nitrogenous wastes;
  2) imparts a taste that is better tolerated than that of chlorine;
  3) is easier to transport;
  4) can double as a topical disinfectant for wound care.

Iodine will not kill Cryptosporidium at concentrations used for disinfecting drinking water, and must be allowed to sit in the water for a longer period of time to kill Giardia.

It takes longer to work in cold water, so the dose or the contact time with the water must be increased. Some iodine is absorbed by impurities in the water, so more is required for cloudy or polluted water. If you add flavoring to the water, make sure to do so only after the iodine has had adequate contact time with the water.

10% POVIDONE IODINE SOLUTION (Betadine®)
Measure with dropper (1 drop = .05 ml)
Add to 1 liter or quart of water

Drops per Liter or Quart	Water Temperature	Water Clarity	Contact Time
8	Warm	Clear	30 Min.
16	Warm	Cloudy	30 Min.
8	Cold	Clear	60 Min.
16	Cold (less than 50F../10C.)	Cloudy	60 Min.

IODINE TABLETS[1]

Tablets per Liter or Quart	Water Temperature	Water Clarity	Contact Time
1	Warm	Clear	15 Min.
2	Warm	Cloudy	15 Min.
1	Cold	Clear	45 Min.
2	Cold	Cloudy	45 Min.

(1) Backer H.: "Field Water Disinfection." In: Wilderness Medicine: Management of Wilderness and Environmental Emergencies, Third Edition, Editor: Auerbach PS, Mosby, 1995.

APPENDIX B

FIRST-AID KITS

A first aid kit is one of the "Ten Essential backcountry Items"; the basic things that EVERYONE should have on EVERY backcountry trip.

When designing a wilderness first-aid kit, you will need to consider several prerequisites and variables. These include:

1. Your medical expertise
2. The location and environmental extremes of your destination
3. Diseases that may be particular to an area of travel
4. The duration of travel
5. The distance you will be from definitive medical care and the availability of professional rescue
6. The number of people the kit will need to support
7. Pre-existing illnesses that someone may have
8. Weight and space limitations

The wilderness medical kit should be well organized in a protective and convenient carrying pouch. For backpacking, trekking or hiking, a nylon organizer bag is optimal. Newer generation bags with clear, protective vinyl compartments have proven superior to mesh-covered pockets. The vinyl protects the components from dirt, moisture and insects and prevents items from falling out when the kit is turned on its side or upside down.

For aquatic environments, the kit should be stored in a waterproof dry bag or water-tight hard container. Inside, items should be sealed in zip-lock bags, since moisture will invariably make its way into any container.

Some medicines may need to be stored outside of the main kit to ensure protection from extreme temperatures. Capsules and suppositories melt when exposed to body temperature heat (99 F), and many liquid medicines become useless after freezing.

For state-of-the-art wilderness first aid kits, contact **Adventure Medical Kits, P.O. Box 43309, Oakland, California, (800) 324-3517.**

EQUIPMENT

- **Sam® Splint**
A versatile and lightweight foam-padded aluminum splint. Adaptable for use on almost any part of the body, it can be fashioned as a cervical collar, arm, leg, or ankle splint.

- **Hypothermia & Hypothermia thermometers**
Ideally should be able to read temperatures down to 85 degrees and up to 107 degrees Fahrenheit.

- **CPR Microshield® or CPR Life Mask Shield®**
Compact and easy to use clear, flexible barriers for performing mouth-to-mouth rescue breathing. Prevents physical contact with the victim's secretions.

- **Bandage scissors**
Designed with a blunt tip to protect the patient while cutting through clothes, boots or bandages.

- **Cotton tipped applicators (Q-tips)**
May be used to remove insects or other foreign material from the eye. Also useful to roll fluid out from beneath a blister, or to evert an eyelid to locate a foreign body.

- **Glutose® Paste**
Oral glucose gel containing concentrated sugar for treating hypoglycemia and insulin reactions in diabetics, and for hypothermia.

- **Safety pins**

- **Duct tape**

- **Accident Report Form**

- **Pencil**

- **Plastic resealable (zip-lock) bags**

WOUND MANAGEMENT ITEMS

- **10-20 cc irrigation syringe with an 18-gauge catheter tip**
  Using the syringe like a squirt gun flushes out germs from wounds without harming the delicate tissues.

- **Povidone iodine solution USP 10% (Betadine®)**
  To disinfect backcountry water and to sterilize wound edges. When diluted 10-fold with water, it can be used for wound irrigation.

- **1/4" by 4" wound closure strips**
  These are excellent for closing cuts in the wilderness. Wound closure strips are stronger, longer, stickier, and more porous than the common butterfly-type adhesive bandages.

- **Tincture of benzoin**
  A liquid adhesive which enhances the stickiness of wound closure strips or tape.

- **Polysporin or double antibiotic ointment**
  A topical antibiotic ointment that helps to prevent minor skin infections and accelerate wound healing. Avoid triple antibiotic ointments with neomycin. They can produce an allergic rash in susceptible individuals.

- **Forceps or tweezers**
  For removing embedded objects from the skin such as splinters, cactus thorns, ticks or stingers

- **First-aid cleansing pads with lidocaine**
  These pads have a textured surface which makes them ideal for scrubbing dirt and embedded objects out of "road rash" abrasions. Lidocaine is a topical anesthetic.

- **Antiseptic towelettes with benzalkonium chloride**
  Disposable wipes that may be use to clean wounds. Benzalkonium chloride may help to kill the rabies virus on wounds inflicted by animals.

- **Surgical scrub brush**
  A sterile scrub brush for cleaning embedded objects and dirt from abrasions.

- **Aloe vera gel**
  A topical anti-inflammatory gel for treating burns, frostbite, abrasions, and poison oak and ivy.

- **Nitrile barrier gloves**
  To protect the rescuer from infectious diseases such as hepatitis and AIDS. Latex gloves can cause serious allergic reactions and should be avoided.

BANDAGE MATERIAL

- **8" x 10" or 5" x 9" sterile trauma pads**
- **4" x 4" sterile dressings**
- **Non-adherent sterile dressings**
  Non-stick dressings are used to cover abrasions, burns, lacerations, and blisters. Some examples include: Aquaphor®, Xeroform®, Adaptic®, and Telfa®. Spenco 2nd Skin® is an excellent alternative and provides an ideal covering for burns, blisters, abrasions, and cuts. It is a polyethylene oxide gel laminate composed of 96% water which cools and soothes on contact and can be left in place for up to 48 hours.

- **Gauze roller bandages or Kling®**
  A sterile bandage that is used to keep the dressing in place and further protect a wound from the environment.

- **Elastic roller bandage or Ace® wrap**
  A bandage used to hold dressings in place or to create a pressure bandage for bleeding, or for sprains.

- **Assortment of strip and knuckle adhesive bandages**

- **Stockinet bandage**
  A net style bandage particularly useful for holding dressings in place across a joint.

- **Molefoam®**
  A thick, padded adhesive material for protecting blisters. Cut a doughnut out of the material and place it around a blister site.

- **Moleskin®**
  A thin, padded adhesive material for protecting skin from developing blisters.

- **Tape**

- **Triangular Bandage**
  Useful for making a sling and swath, holding splints in place, or improvising a foot harness for a traction splint.

NON-PRESCRIPTION MEDICATIONS

WARNING: A physician should be consulted before any tor nursing mother. Read the instructions carefully on the medication package and do not use if you think you may be allergic to the drug.

IBUPROFEN (Motrin®)

Indications: For the temporary relief of minor aches and pains associated with the common cold, headache, toothache, muscular aches, backache, and arthritis. Also effective in reducing the inflammation associated with sprains, strains, bursitis, tendonitis, minor burns, and frostbite. Reduces the pain of menstrual cramps and lowers fever.

Dosage: Adults: 400 to 800 mg every eight hours with food. Do not take on an empty stomach. Children: Ibuprofen is available by prescription in a liquid form for children.

WARNING: Do not take Ibuprofen if you are allergic to aspirin or any other non-steroidal anti-inflammatory drug. It may cause upset stomach or heartburn. Do not use if you have gastritis, ulcers or are prone to bleeding or on any blood thinner medication. Not recommended for use during pregnancy. Avoid if you have kidney disease.

ACETAMINOPHEN (Tylenol®)

Indications: For relief of pain and fever. Tylenol has no anti-inflammatory effect.

Dosage: Adults: 1000 mg every four to six hours. Children: 15 mg/kg every four to six hours.

WARNING: In case of overdose, contact a physician or poison control center immediately. Do not use this drug if you have any liver disease, or if you regularly consume alcohol. Avoid if you have an allergy to this medicine.

DIPHENHYDRAMINE (Benadryl®)

Indications: Diphenhydramine is an antihistamine that can temporarily relieve runny nose, sneezing, watery eyes, and itchy throat due to hay fever or other respiratory allergies and colds. Relieves itching and rash associated with allergic reactions, and poison oak or ivy. Useful as an adjunct to epinephrine in the treatment of severe allergic shock. May also prevent and help relieve the symptoms of motion sickness.

Dosage: Adults: 25 to 50 mg every four to six hours. Children: consult your physician.

WARNING: May cause drowsiness. Individuals with asthma, glaucoma, high blood pressure, emphysema, or prostatic enlargement should not use unless directed by a physician. Not recommended for use in hot environments, when heat illness is likely, during pregnancy, or while taking other anti-cholinergic medications (consult your physician before use).

ALOE VERA GEL

Indications: A topical treatment for first-degree and second-degree burns, frostbite, abrasions and blisters.

Dosage: apply a thin coat to the effected area two to three times a day.

WARNING: Discontinue use if redness, swelling or pain develop at the site.

HYDROCORTISONE CREAM USP 1%

Indications: For temporary relief of minor skin irritations and allergic reaction.

Dosage: Adults and children two years of age and older: apply to affected area not more than three to four times a day. Children under two: consult a physician.

WARNING: If condition worsens or if symptoms persist for more than seven days or clear up and occur again within a few days, stop use of this product and do not begin use of any other hydrocortisone product unless you have consulted a physician. Do not use for the treatment of diaper rash. In case of accidental ingestion seek professional assistance or contact a poison control center immediately. Keep this and all drugs out of the reach of children. For external use only. Avoid contact with eyes.

ALUMINUM HYDROXIDE AND SIMETHICONE TABLETS
(Mylanta®)

Indications: Each tablet contains both an antacid and an anti-gas ingredient. Helps relieve heartburn, acid indigestion, sour stomach, and gas. Provides symptomatic relief of peptic ulcer disease and gastritis.

Dosage: Two to four tablets between meals and at bedtime.

WARNING: Do not use Mylanta if you have kidney disease. It can interfere with the absorption of certain antibiotics. If symptoms persist, consult a physician as soon as possible.

ORAL REHYDRATION SALT PACKETS
(electrolyte salts and glucose)

When combined with a quart of water, they provide an ideal solution for replacing electrolytes and fluids lost during diarrhea illness, heat exhaustion or vomiting.

RECOMMENDED PRESCRIPTION MEDICATION

WARNING: A physician should be consulted before any medication is taken by a child, pregnant woman, or nursing mother. Make sure that you are not allergic to any drugs that you plan to use. Sharing medications with others is potentially hazardous and is not recommended. Do not treat yourself or others unless there is no alternative and you are comfortable with the problem. Doses listed are for adults only. Carefully review the dose, indications, and adverse effects of all drugs that you plan to carry.

EPI E•Z PEN® (EPINEPHRINE AUTO-INJECTOR) & EPI E•Z PEN® JR.

Epinephrine quickly constricts blood vessels and relaxes smooth muscles. It improves breathing, stimulates the heart to beat faster and harder, and relieves hives and swelling.

Indication: Emergency treatment of severe allergic reactions (anaphylaxis) to bees, wasps, hornets, yellow jackets, foods, drugs, and other allergens. May also help relieve symptoms of asthma.

Dosage:
For adults and children over 66 lbs: .Each Epi E•Z Pen® contains 2 ml of epinephrine 1:1000 USP in a disposable push button spring activated cartridge with a concealed needle. It will deliver a single dose of 0.3 mg epineph-rine intramuscularly. Pull off the cap and place the black tip against the thigh. Press the gray button on top of the auto-injector down with your thumb to release a spring activated plunger, and push a concealed needle into the thigh muscle. The drug should be felt within one to two minutes. For children who weigh less than 66 lbs. The Epi E•Z Pen® Jr. will deliver a single dose of 0.15 mg of epinephrine.

WARNING: Epinephrine should be avoided in individuals who are older than 50 years of age, or who have a known heart condition, unless the situation is life-threatening. Sometimes a single dose of epinephrine may not be enough to completely reverse the effects of an anaphylac-tic reaction. For individuals who know they have severe allergic reactions, it may be wise to carry more than one auto-injector.

ANTIBIOTICS

Some of the antibiotics listed below have similar uses and overlapping spectrums of antibacterial activity. Before departing on your trip, discuss with your physician which antibiotics best suit your needs.

AZITHROMYCIN (ZITHROMAX®) 250 MG CAPSULES

This is a broad-spectrum, erythromycin-type antibiotic. It is more potent than erythromycin, causes fewer side-effects, and only has to be taken once a day for five days.

Indications: Tonsillitis, ear infections, bronchitis, pneumonia, sinusitis, traveler's diarrhea, skin infections.

Dosage: Take two capsules on the first day, followed by one capsule a day for four more days.

WARNING: Do not use if you are allergic to erythromycin. Do use simultaneously with the antihistamines Seldane® or Hismanal®.

AMOXICILLIN CLAVULANATE (AUGMENTIN®) 500 MG TABLETS

A broad-spectrum penicillin-type antibiotic.

Indications: Bite wounds, skin infections, pneumonia, urinary tract infections, ear infections, bronchitis, tonsillitis and sinusitis.

Dosage: One tablet every eight hours, for seven to ten days.

WARNING: Do not use if allergic to penicillin. Stop use if rash develops. May cause diarrhea.

CIPROFLOXACIN (CIPRO®) 500 MG TABLETS

An excellent antibiotic for traveler's diarrhea and dysentery.

Indications: Diarrhea, pneumonia, urinary tract infections, bone infections.

Dosage: One tablet twice a day, for three days. For kidney infections, pneumonia and bone infections, treat for seven to ten days.

WARNING: Not recommended for patients less than 18 years old or pregnant or nursing women. Adverse effects, although uncommon, have included nausea, vomiting, diarrhea, and abdominal pain.

ERYTHROMYCIN 250/500 MG TABLETS

An alternative antibiotic for individuals allergic to penicillin.
   Indications: Bronchitis, tonsillitis, pneumonia, skin infections, sinus infections, ear, and eye infections.
   Dosage: 250-500 mg every six hours, for seven to ten days.
   WARNING: May cause upset stomach, vomiting, and/or diarrhea. Take with food.

CEFUROXIME (CEFTIN®) OR CEPHALEXIN (KEFLEX®) 250 TO 500 MG TABLETS

Broad-spectrum antibiotics which can be substituted for Augmentin®, in individuals allergic to penicillin.
   Indications: Skin infections, bronchitis, urinary tract infections, tonsillitis, middle ear infections, some bone infections, bite wounds, tonsillitis, dental infections, sinusitis.
   Dosage: 250-500 mg every six hours.
   WARNING: Avoid or use with caution in individuals with penicillin allergy, since 5% of people may be cross-reactive.

METRONIDAZOLE (FLAGYL®). 250 MG TABLETS

   Indications: Intra-abdominal infections including peritonitis and appendicitis, dental infections.
   Dosage: Intra-abdominal infections: two tablets every six hours if the patient is not vomiting.
   WARNING: Do not drink alcohol while taking this medication. The interaction will cause severe abdominal pain, nausea, and vomiting. May cause unpleasant metallic taste. Do not use during pregnancy.

NITAZOXANIDE (ALINIA®). 500 MG TABLETS
Indications: Giardia and Cryptosporidiosis.
Dosage: The adult dose is 500 mg twice a day for three days. The dose in children is 100 mg twice a day for three days.

TRIMETHOPRIM/SULFAMETHOXAZOLE
Common brand names include Septra DS® and Bactrim DS®. Each tablet contains 80 mg trimethoprim and 400 mg sulfamethoxazole.
Indications: Urinary tract or kidney infections, ear and sinus infections, and bronchitis. Can be substituted for ciprofloxacin to treat traveler's diarrhea or dysentery. It is cheaper than ciprofloxacin, but some bacteria which cause dysentery have developed resistance to this drug.
Dosage: One tablet twice a day for five days for diarrhea and dysentery. Other infections may require a ten-day course.
WARNING: Do not use in individuals allergic to sulfa drugs. Trimethoprim 200 mg alone, twice a day, may be substituted for treatment of diarrhea and dysentery. Discontinue use at the first sign of skin rash or any adverse reaction. Do not use in pregnancy.

LEVOFLOXACIN (LEVAQUIN®) 500 MG TABLETS
Indications: Bronchitis, pneumonia, urinary tract infections, sinusitis, skin infections, anthrax.
Dosage: 500 mg every 24 hours for 7-14 days.

CORTISPORIN® OTIC SUSPENSION
Indications: External ear infections ("Swimmer's Ear")
Dosage: Four drops instilled into the affected ear four times a day.
WARNING: Discontinue using if a rash develops or the condition worsens.

FOR NAUSEA AND VOMITING

COMPAZINE® OR PHENERGAN® SUPPOSITORIES
Indications: For control of severe nausea and vomiting.

Dosage: 25 mg rectally twice a day.
WARNING: Do not use in children. Side effects include neck spasm, difficulty in swallowing and talking, sensation that the tongue is thick, muscle stiffness, and agitation. If these symptoms occur, discontinue use of the drug and administer Benadryl® 50 mg. May produce drowsiness.

ONDANSETRON (ZOFRAN ODT®) 4 MG
Indications: For control of severe nausea and vomiting.
Dosage: Place 4 mg tablet on tongue immediately after opening blister pack and allow it to dissolve. Handle with dry hands. Do not cut/chew tablet.

SYMPTOMATIC RELIEF OF DIARRHEA

IMODIUM® 2 MG CAPSULE *(available over-the-counter)*
Indications: For controlling the abdominal cramping and diarrhea associated with intestinal infections.
Dosage: 4 mg initially, followed by one capsule (2 mg) after each loose bowel movement not to exceed 14 mg in one day.
WARNING: Imodium® should not be used if there is associated fever (greater than 101 F), blood or pus in the stool, or the abdomen becomes swollen. It should not be used for more than 48 hours. Do not give this drug to children.

PEPTO-BISMOL® *(available over-the-counter)*
Each tablet contains 262 mg bismuth subsalicylate.
Indications: May prevent and help treat traveler's diarrhea, nausea, and upset stomach.
Dosage: Two tablets four times a day.
WARNING: This medication should not be used by individuals allergic to aspirin. Children and teenagers who have or are recovering from chicken pox or flu should not use to treat vomiting. If vomiting occurs, consult a physician as this could be an early sign of Reyes Syndrome, a rare but serious illness. As with any drug, if you are pregnant or nursing a baby, seek the advice of a health professional before using.

EYE INFECTIONS

TOBREX® OPTHALMIC SOLUTION 0.3%
A topical antibiotic for the eye.
>   *Indications:* For external infections of the eye (conjunctivitis or pink eye, or corneal abrasions).
>   *Dosage:* One to two drops into the affected eye every two hours while awake.
>   WARNING: Do not use if you develop or have an allergy or sensitivity to this medicine.

PAIN MEDICATION

VICODIN®
>   Each tablet contains hydrocodone 5 mg and acetaminophen 500 mg.
>   *Indications:* For relief of pain. Can also be used for relief of diarrhea and suppression of coughs.
>   *Dosage:* One to two tablets every four to six hours.
>   WARNING: Codeine is a narcotic and may be habit forming. Side effects include drowsiness, respiratory depression, constipation, and nausea. Do not use if allergic to either acetaminophen or codeine.

ALTITUDE ILLNESS

ACETEZOLAMIDE (DIAMOX®) 250 MG TABLETS
>   *Indications:* May help to prevent altitude illness when used in conjunction with graded ascent and to treat altitude illness in conjunction with descent. Useful in diminishing the sleep disorder associated with mountain sickness.
>   *Dosage:* For prevention, 125 mg (1/2 tablet) twice a day, beginning the day before the ascent. For treatment, 250 mg twice a day until symptoms resolve.
>   WARNING: Diamox is not a substitute for graded ascent and acclimatization, nor a substitute for descent in the event of severe altitude illness. Side effects include increased

urination, numbness in the fingers and toes, and lethargy. Carbonated beverages will also taste terrible. Do not use if allergic to sulfa medications.

DEXAMETHASONE (DECADRON®)

Indications: For the treatment of High Altitude Cerebral Edema (HACE) in conjunction with immediate descent to a lower altitude.

Dosage: 8 mg initially, followed by 4 mg every six hours.

NIFEDIPINE (PROCARDIA®)

Indications: For the treatment of High Altitude Pulmonary Edema (HAPE) in conjunction with immediate descent to a lower altitude.

Dosage: 10 mg every four hours or 10 mg one time, followed by 30 mg extended release capsule every 12 to 24 hours.

WARNING: May cause low blood pressure and fainting, especially when standing up from a lying position.

BASIC DENTAL KIT

- **Dental floss**
- **Cavit® temporary filling material**
- **Cotton rolls**
- **Zinc oxide**
- **Eugenol (oil of cloves)**
- **Cotton pellets**

Mixing together zinc oxide and eugenol will make a temporary filling, which sets in a few minutes after contact with saliva

MEDICAL SUPPLIES FOR
EXTENDED EXPEDITIONS

- Foley catheter

- Airway supplies (oral or nasal airways, endotracheal and cricothyrodotomy tubes)

- Advanced wound management supplies
  1. Suture set and suture material
  2. Surgical staples
  3. 1% xylocaine for anesthesia

- Intravenous solutions and administration tubing

- Needles and syringes

- Urine chemstrips for diagnosing urinary tract infections

- Urine pregnancy test

Marine Environment
- 5% acetic acid (vinegar)
- Prednisone

Cold Environment
- Low reading (down to at least 85 degrees) thermometer
- Matches
- Glutose® paste (concentrated sugar to help the body generate heat)

Jungle or third world travel
- Oral rehydration salt packets

- Antibiotics for treating "traveler's diarrhea" (ciprofloxacin or azithromycin)

- Loperamide (Imodium®) for symptomatic relief of diarrhea

- Clotrimazole or betamethasone dipropionate cream (Lo-trisone®) for treating fungal infections

- Permethrin 5% cream and 1% shampoo for treating lice, bedbugs and scabies

- Insect repellent

APPENDIX C

INTERNET INFORMATION RESOURCES FOR TRAVELERS

World Health Organization Home Page:
www.who.int/home-page

WHO Travel and International Health Information Site
www.who.int/ith/index.html

**US Centers for Disease Control and Prevention
- Travel Medicine**
Home Page: www.cdc.gov/travel/index.html

US Centers for Disease Control, Office of Global Health
www.cdc.gov/ogh

**US State Department Travel Warnings and Consular
Information** www.travel.state.gov/travel_warnings.html

Divers Alert Network (DAN): www.diversalertnetwork.org

Travel Health On-Line (Shoreland, Inc.):
www.tripprep.com

International Association for Medical Assistance to Travelers (IAMAT): www.iamat.org

MASTA (Australia): www.masta.edu.au/

MASTA (England): www.masta.org/home.html

TRAVEL CLINIC DIRECTORIES

ISTM: www.istm.org/disclinics.html

ASTM&H: www.astmh.org/clinics/clinindex.html

Lonely Planet Health:
www.lonelyplanet.com/health/health.htm

INDEX

The Choice of Outdoor Professionals Worldwide

Since 1987 Adventure Medical Kits mission has been to provide travelers and outdoor adventurers with the most comprehensive and innovative first aid kits and medical information available. In 2005 we are proud to publish Dr. Weiss' third edition of *A Comprehensive Guide to Wilderness and Travel Medicine*. Our collaborations with medical professionals such as Dr. Weiss, who are experts in their fields, allow us to meet our mission statement and in the end provide you with the resources and information you need to enjoy a safe and healthy trip.

Safe Adventures,

The Team at Adventure Medical Kits

For more information on our comprehensive line of medical kits, survival gear, insect protection and treatment and to get up-to-date medical information and tips, please visit: **www.adventuremedicalkits.com**

Adventure Medical Kits
P.O. Box 43309 • Oakland, CA 94624 • 510-261-7414